Cowboy Collectibles and Western Memorabilia

Robert W.D. Ball and Ed Vebell

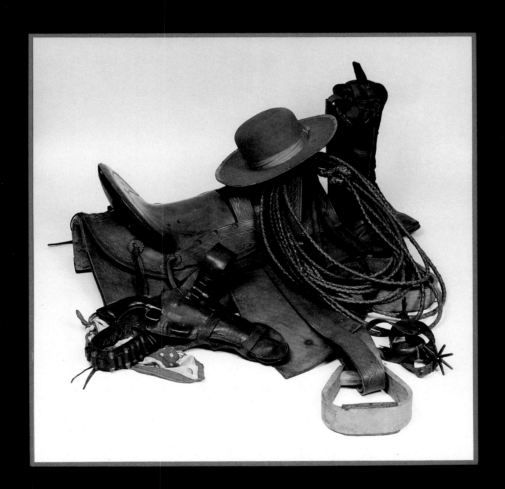

1469 Morstein Road, West Chester, Pennsylvania 19380

Acknowledgements

Our most heartfelt thanks go to those friends, strangers (and now good friends!), dealers, avid collectors, and curators without whom this book would still be in the gestation period. We have tried to show every item to its best advantage and describe each piece as exactly as possible. It is our sincere wish that we have satisfied even the most ardent collector.

David Corrigan, Curator, Museum of Connecticut History

Steve Crowley

Dr. Deborah Ducoff-Barone, Museum of Connecticut History

Robert Dailey, Harwinton, Connecticut

Michael L Gardner Photography, Ashford, Connecticut

Jerard Paul Jordan Galleries, Ashford, Connecticut

Jonathan M. Peck, Avon, Connecticut

Don Spaulding

Windsor Arms Company, Larry Kaufman, Windsor, Connecticut

Printed in the United States of America.
ISBN: 0-88740-329-8

Published by Schiffer Publishing, Ltd.
1469 Morstein Road
West Chester, Pennsylvania 19380
Please write for a free catalog.
This book may be purchased from the publisher.
Please include $2.00 postage.
Try your bookstore first.

We are interested in hearing from authors with book ideas on related subjects.

Title Page Photo: Group of saddle, hat, lariat, boots, spurs, holstered pistol, and bandanna. *Don Spaulding.*

Front Cover Photo: Cabinet photo of buckskin clad hunter with shotgun and pistol. Denver, Colorado. Group showing saddle, lariat, boots, spurs, holstered pistol, and bandanna. *Don Spaulding.*

Back Cover Photo: Cabinet photo of Algernon Smith, 7th Cavalry. Vertical view of Cavalry artifacts, including a Model 1872 cavalry officer's dress helmet, Captain Benteen's pistol, flask, knife, box of pistol cartridges, field belt with knife and sheath, carte-de-visite of General George A. Custer, all grouped around the field chest of Captain George Yates of the 7th Cavalry. *Don Spaulding.*

Spine: Pinch Frame Cavalry Model Colt .45 Single Action revolver, Serial number 48. *Jonathan Peck.*

Contents

Illustration by Ed Vebell for the Postal Commemorative Society, "Homestead Act."

Foreword

Hunched in the saddle under a broiling sun, shivering in the midst of a driving blizzard, days on horseback moving cattle, poor food, little money and countless boring hours....all were the lot of the cowboy on the western frontier during the last century. Usually drifting from job to job, owning not much more than his saddle, horse, weapon and what he could carry in his bedroll, these men were bigger than life then and remain bigger than life even now.

In childhood many of us had an interest, nurtured by films and novels, of the early cowboy roaming the range, herding cattle, breaking broncs, and fighting Indians and cattle rustlers. "The cowboy was far more than a theatric character. He was an affirmative, constructive factor in the social and political development of the United States."[1] As we grew older, that interest intensified into collecting cowboy and western gear that would remind us of that rugged and nostalgic time.

At home and abroad, individuals and museums have painstakingly accumulated items of every description relating to the early western settlers, including rifles, pistols, saddles, clothing, boots, hats, blankets, gun rigs, and even barbed wire, anything at all that glamorizes the American cowboy. It is the hope of the authors that by picture and word, we can contribute to the preservation of this unique era of Americana.

These pages contain examples of the gear the ordinary cowpoke used, wore, rode upon, ate from, and slept under. While becoming increasingly scarce, much of the equipment and clothing shown here can still be found at reasonable prices, if one is willing to search the antique shops, the flea markets, and the tag sales in small out-of-the-way Western towns.

Illustration by Ed Vebell for the Postal Commemorative Society, "Promontory Point, Utah."

Introduction

Cabinet photo of a 7th Cavalry officer.

In the 1600s and well into the 1700s, the western portion of this continent was an unknown and mysterious stretch of country. Most was familiar only to those nomadic tribes who had staked out territories through centuries of wandering and war-like depredations against other tribes. The land was virginal, overflowing with teeming herds of wild animals, lush prairies of sweet grasses, and abundant supplies of fresh water. The native inhabitants of this beautiful place took only what they needed of the fruits of the earth, and killed only to provide the food needed to survive.

From the territories of the Spanish Conquistadors south of the Rio Grande, small parties of explorers, frequently accompanied by men of the cloth, made many perilous and often tragic journeys north to the unexplored lands that beckoned them. Missions were established and trading posts were set up nearby, but many were wiped out in raids by Indians resentful of the Spaniards' intrusion into their native lands. Rarely deterred by the destruction around them, missions and settlements were doggedly rebuilt and the work of colonization continued. It took the gold rush of 1849, however, to trigger the population explosion in what is now known as California. In the meantime, the lands that later became Texas, Arizona, and New Mexico were being worked by the Spaniards and Mexicans, who traded and frequently intermarried with the Indians, mined voraciously, and built ranches and raised cattle on a scale that now seems unimaginable.

Concurrent with early developments in the West, the eastern coast of the country was being settled by people from Europe, mainly Great Britain, who established colonies from what is now South Carolina to the Maine grants. By the early 1700s, the expansion westward had begun. There were settlers looking for free lands, explorers with an insatiable curiosity about what awaited them over the next mountain, and frontiersmen stifled by the crush of civilization. By slow degrees, a steady western movement of pioneers continued right through the Oklahoma land rush in the early 1900s.

In 1804, the Lewis and Clark expedition began its exploration of what is now the northwestern United States. In its footsteps came the trappers and hunters, carving out their niche in history. And in their wake came the first settlers.

From small beginnings the ranches of the future were built; sparse groups of cattle became the vast herds that eventually covered thousands of acres of grazing land as settlements moved steadily across the country. From the rapidly industrializing East, the railroads began to push farther and farther west, opening up new and broader markets to both cattlemen and the eastern consumer.

Coupled with this expansion was the tremendous increase in immigration from the countries of Europe, with people fleeing oppression and staking all for the opportunity to make a new life for themselves. Many of them remained in the East only long enough to board a train heading for the western territories. From these newly landed immigrants, from others who longed for their own stake in the lands of the West, and from those who were born on the frontier and raised in the saddle, sprang the breed of man known as the cowboy, destined to fill a need, get the job done, and do the job right.

Though the cowboy generally was not one to complain about his day-to-day life, it was bitterly hard at worst and had little to brag about at best. The work was demanding and full of dangers. Even when there was time for relaxation, there was not much in the way of entertainment in the territories during the post-Civil War years. When the cowboys were able to get to the widely scattered frontier towns with some pay in their pockets, games of chance, liquor, and prostitutes (not necessarily in that order) seemed the best of choices for them. In the bunkhouse at the ranch, after the endless chores to be done, the cowboy found time to make things for himself, relaxing by braiding a reata or personalizing some cuffs or gauntlets for his working outfit.

The high point of the cowboy story starts during the time of the Civil War and continues to the beginning of the present century. This was a time of great changes in the West —and a time when the cowboy became the figure that we idealize today.

A beautifully decorated, squaw-made, fringed buckskin jacket for a white man.

Clothing of the Old West

Other than clothes for special occasions, the cowboy had little choice in the garments he wore. With very few exceptions, every item of clothing had a utilitarian purpose.

In Texas and the border states, canvas work coats were often worn for protection on the trail. The coat was usually light brown in color, with skirts to the knee, and, to make it completely wind proof, was given a generous exterior coat of paint. Weather conditions in the more northerly territories mandated heavier, thigh length fur coats made of bearskin, sheepskin or horsehide. Both styles often would be flannel-lined for added warmth and protection.

Wool pants, as well as canvas Levis, were frequently reinforced with leather at the seat and down the inside of the thighs in order to prevent the pants from fraying

An outstanding example of a brain-tanned, squaw-made buckskin jacket and trousers with detailed quill work on the chest pockets as well as the trousers. Circa 1870.

and prematurely wearing out from contact with the saddle leathers. Belts were only worn infrequently, so pants had to fit rather snugly around the waist.

Shirts, for the most part collarless, were flannel or wool, with the choice of colors limited to shades of grey, brown, and black. Shirts might be checked, striped, or solid colored, but were almost never red. Red was reputed to go badly among the cattle, though it was considered the color of choice of miners. The cowboy's taste in colors was quite subdued and garments were almost universally somber in hue.

The vests—really a sleeveless coat—was the handiest item of clothing. It was worn not as a piece of clothing, but solely because its outside pockets provided handy storage. When on horseback it is almost impossible to reach a hand into a pant's pocket, especially if chaps are being worn, so the cowboy insisted that the vest had roomy pockets to carry his essentials. The vest was usually left unbuttoned.

Bandannas were multi-purpose items. They were worn over the mouth as dust filters, used as bandages or slings in a time of need, blindfolds for a horse, handy towels, or to secure a hat during a storm. Everyday bandannas were made of brightly dyed cotton, while expensive silk neckerchiefs were bought for those special occasions in a cowboy's life, like community meetings, dances, and picnics. Storekeepers followed the line of least resistance and, with no special requests for green, blue, or whatever, only stocked the ubiquitous red bandanna, which wasn't offensive to cowboy *or* cattle.

Details of exquisite quill work on a white man's squaw-made jacket of trousers.

Squaw-made fringed buckskin shirt, dated to the 1880 period by the high collar. Could have been worn by an Indian man.

Buckskin jacket with fringed chest and trousers, made for either a cavalry officer or a scout.

Buckskin fringed jacket which was probably made for a scout. This design is typical of the 1870s.

Close-up of the detail on the chest of the buckskin jacket. Please note the Civil War buttons that were used.

A great hide shirt from the 1870s, with quill work on the chest placket and collar. *Don Spaulding.*

Wonderful old trapper's coat, circa 1840 to 1860. Hide laced, with large bone buttons. See how the bottom of the sleeves are dark from being immersed in water during beaver trapping. Note also the large collar reminiscent of early caped coats of the Post-Revolutionary War style. Shown with contemporary skinning knife and trade axe with the original haft. *Don Spaulding.*

Hide coat decorated on the collar, shoulders, pockets, and back with Eastern Sioux quill work. Note the wide elbows as found only on Civil War era coats. Circa 1860s. *Don Spaulding.*

Squaw-made hide coat, made for white men. Typical of coats worn by scouts on the plains. Circa 1870. *Don Spaulding.*

Typical early frontiersman's hide shirt. Note how the placket, pockets, collar, sleeves and cuffs are lined with trade cloth. *Don Spaulding.*

Superb hide trapper's coat, by all accounts from the Great Lakes region. Note the beaded decorations and the Hudson Bay Company buttons. *Don Spaulding.*

Hide trousers that go with the frontiersman's shirt. Note how trade cloth was used to edge the legs and the waist band and see the brown canvas-like lining. *Don Spaulding.*

The same trousers showing the brown canvas-like lining. *Don Spaulding.*

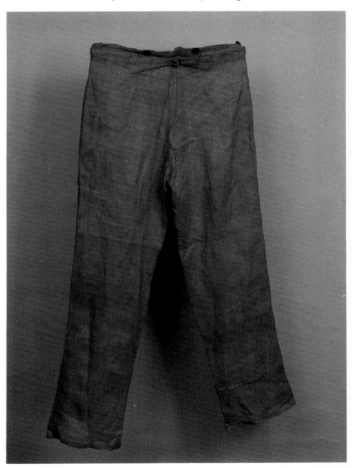

Blue jeans from the 1880s. Note the button fly and the suspender buttons. *Don Spaulding.*

Linen trousers from the 1870s. *Don Spaulding.*

Rear view of the same blue jeans, showing the strap and buckle in the back. *Don Spaulding.*

Rear view of the linen trousers showing the strap and buckle for size adjustment. *Don Spaulding.*

Cotton flannel work shirt of the 1860s. Note the dropped shoulders and the Civil War era buttons. *Don Spaulding*.

A work shirt from the turn-of-the-century. *Don Spaulding*.

Two shirts worn by Tom Mix, movie star of the 1930s. Harold Winfield Scott, a western pulp magazine artist was sketching at the Madison Square rodeo in New York City. Upon seeing the sketches, Tom Mix swapped two of his shirts in exchange for the artwork.

(Left) Polka dot vest, circa 1860.
(Right) Solid color vest from the
1850s. This is determined by the
laced ties on the back of the vest.
In the pocket of the vest is an
"Uhlinger" Pocket Model pistol
with spur trigger. *Don Spaulding.*

(Left) A small patterned vest from the
1870s. (Right) Plaid vest, circa 1860. *Don
Spaulding.*

Two vests from the 1870s,
the one on the right has a
pouch of cut plug tobacco in
the pocket. The pocket of the
vest on the left contains a
watch. *Don Spaulding.*

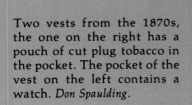

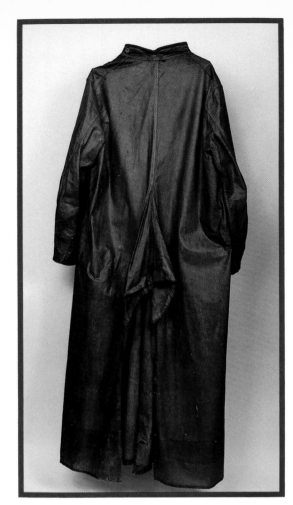

Rear view of the cowboy slicker showing the gores in the rear to cover the saddle. *Don Spaulding.*

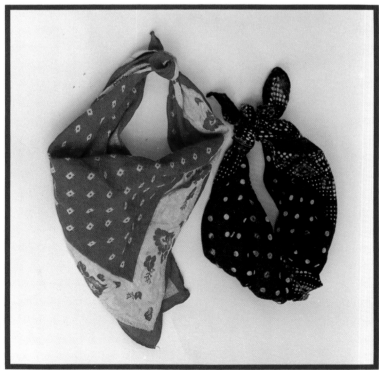

Front view of a rare surviving cowboy slicker. The label reads "Tower's Fish Brand Pommel Slicker, Made in Boston." The color is lined with coarse blue wool. The buttons are arranged in two positions, one for riding and the other for walking. Originally yellow, the color has aged to a copper tone. *Don Spaulding.*

While any differences are not readily obvious, these bandannas are from 1920. *Don Spaulding.*

Three original bandannas from 1865-1870, showing that while the predominant color was red, there were different designs available. *Don Spaulding.*

Fine, original buffalo coat, over 100 years old. Blanket lined, with two chest "slip-in" pockets, and two flapped pockets below. Double row of buttons with loop closures. Note the closely sheared collar fur.

A heavy buffalo coat, incorporating frog type closures. Circa 1880. *Don Spaulding.*

Stocking cap from the 1840s. *Don Spaulding*.

As worn in the West, a man's top hat from the era 1850 to 1860. *Don Spaulding*.

Hats

The one item of apparel that all cowboys had in common was the hat. All manner and shapes of hats were worn in the West, from derbies to Stetsons to sombreros. So attached was the cowpoke to his hat that it became natural in the West for the hat to be worn indoors at all times and places, including in bed!

The hat was another of the frontiers' useful tools, not only shading the head from the sun, rain, or snow, but protecting it, as well, from thorn trees and low hanging branches. If a fire required fanning, or water needed to be carried, the problem was solved with the ever-present and versatile hat.

Around the crown, just above the brim and for the purpose of regulating the fit of the hat, ran an adjustable belt. It was usually made of leather, but is sometimes found made of woven silver or gold wire. If in leather, it was commonly ornamented with metal studs or, if money allowed, silver "conchas" in the form of flat metal plates. A rattlesnake's skin was sometimes substituted for the leather belt.

Although subject to variations, there appear to have been four identifiable styles of hats in the West.

The *Sugar-loaf Sombrero*, was high peaked with a broad brim that offered great protection from the sun, It was often worn with a horsehair braided band.

The *Plainsman*, was usually low-crowned with a floppy brim and tie strings, and was ideally suited for windy ranges. These were preferred by the early vaqueros, who later adopted the high peaked "Stetson Yankee," produced by the manufacturer whose name was almost synonymous with cowboy hats. This Stetson style was often found in the Northwest.

A third style was the *Montana Peak* hat, somewhat of a misnomer since the dented-peak hat was most often found in the Southwest. With its four-sided peak and stiff brim, it is very similar to the drill instructor's hat of today.

The fourth identifiable style was the *Texas* hat, which had a high, uncreased crown and a side-rolled brim. A point of interest was the star that was usually cut into the crown of the *Texas* hat.

Whether a hat was uncreased, creased, rolled brim or stiff was dependent on the time, region, and prevailing style. Most old hats were not maker-marked after the turn of the century, usually showing only the retailer's name. As with any item of attire that is subjected to hard wear and the elements, the collector will have a difficult time finding authentic pre-1900 hats for his collection.

Early—presumably pre-Civil War—broad flat-brimmed hat as used on the frontier.

Bound brim "Sugar Loaf" crown cowboy hat, circa 1860-1870 *Don Spaulding.*

A typical broad brimmed cowboy hat from the 1870s. *Don Spaulding.*

A wonderful example of an early Stetson, with a "Sugar Loaf" crown, dating from 1860-1870. Excellent condition.

Flat-brimmed "Sugar Loaf" crowned hat, circa 1870-1880.

Man's straw hat, circa 1870-1880. *Don Spaulding.*

An example of an early Stetson with a bound brim, shown with either a snake or lizard skin band, as well as with just the original bow. This hat was used in Harold Winfield Scott's "pulp" western covers during the 1930s.

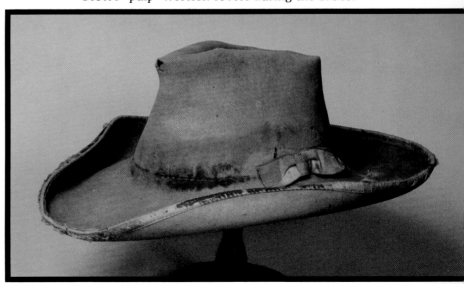

A great man's straw hat from the 1880s. Note the Mexican-style of decorated border. *Don Spaulding*.

A Mexican straw hat, circa 1890, most likely for a landowner or "patron."

Another in the ordinary style of western hats affected by cowpunchers. Circa 1890.

Stockman's style of hat with the curled brim, circa 1890.

A typical 1900s period broad, flat-brimmed western hat as used by the cowboys.

A type of hat favored by the cowboys, circa 1890. *Don Spaulding*.

Black flat-brimmed western hat.

Well-worn cowboy's hat, circa 1900.

Turn-of-the-century western "Sugar Loaf" crown and flat stiff brimmed hat with silk ribbon band.

Heavily used turn-of-the-century western hat acquired by Ed Vebell from Harold Winfield Scott, a Western "pulp" magazine illustrator during the 1930s.

Classic western style hat from around the turn of the century. *Jonathan Peck.*

A turn-of-the-century man's straw hat. *Don Spaulding.*

Two well-used hats, the one on the left was worn by Eric von Schmidt, while the one on the right was worn by his brother, Pete von Schmidt. They were the sons of Harold von Schmidt, the famous western illustrator, and served as his models throughout their lives.

A well-worn cowboy hat from the early 1900s. *Don Spaulding.*

A wonderful find is this hat of a Mexican general, decorated in gold bullion. This was given to Clarence Buddington Clelland, a well-known writer for the *Saturday Evening Post*, by Pancho Villa in 1916. Later, it was given to Harold Winfield Scott, the famous western pulp magazine illustrator. *Don Spaulding.*

An interesting piece of history, this hat was used in the Tom Mix Wild West Show, probably in London, England, with the riders recruited from Texas. The hats were made from World War One military hats, and individually decorated by the individual cowboys.

Recently found hat of nutria fur, with a scrap of paper inside stating that this hat was purchased from Buffalo Bill in 1912 for $10.00 in Joplin, Missouri. The Buffalo Bill Museum believes the hat to have been owned and worn by Buffalo Bill.

Classic Western-style hat.

Mexican woven straw sombrero, usually worn only by Mexican cattlemen. Each state in Mexico had it's own distinctive style of sombrero.

Western hat with the brim curled to give added strength.

As a comparison, this is a modern day western hat as worn by Burt Reynolds, the actor, during one of his cowboy movies.

(Left) 1840s style quilted winter bonnet. (Right) Coal scuttle style bonnet of the 1830s. *Don Spaulding.*

(Left) Straw bonnet with green silk ribbon and artificial flowers. (Right) 1860s bonnet with silk ribbon and lace decoration on buckram base. *Don Spaulding.*

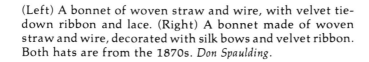

(Left) A bonnet of woven straw and wire, with velvet tie-down ribbon and lace. (Right) A bonnet made of woven straw and wire, decorated with silk bows and velvet ribbon. Both hats are from the 1870s. *Don Spaulding.*

(Left) Checked gingham bonnet. (Right) Sun bonnet. Both bonnets are typical of the 1870s. *Don Spaulding.*

The winter fur hat and gloves, above, were welcome on a frigid day. The hat has the fold down ear flaps, and the gloves' cuffs are extra deep.

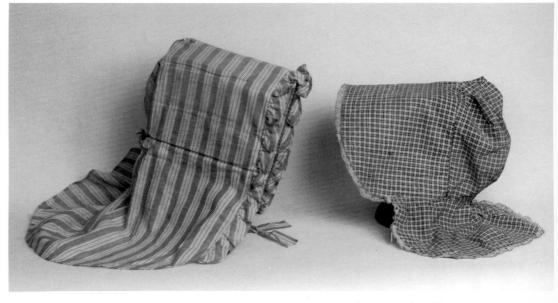

(Left) Early Slat bonnet with long shoulder covering. (Right) Pioneer style sun bonnet. *Don Spaulding.*

Still serviceable boots circa 1864-1870. Note that the fronts were made of one piece of leather and then shaped.

Boots from the early 1870s, found with only one spur remaining. *Don Spaulding.*

Boots with their fronts made of one piece. Circa 1870.

Boots

In the post-Civil War era, many men on the western frontier were fortunate enough to own a pair of cavalry boots brought home from their service with either the North or the South. Others bought boots turned out by early bootmakers like Hyer of Kansas, Justin in Texas, or boots by Frye, one of the original western bootmakers. Later, a favorite on the frontier was the "Coffeyville" boot out of Kansas.

The boots of the 1880s had a square cut vamp (the boot front), high loose square cut "stove pipe" top, and high heels. Usually made of calfskin, they came to just below the knee, with the top of the boot stitched in rows or patterns to stiffen it. The boot protected the leg from stones, thorns, and snakes, while keeping the stirrup leathers from rubbing the calf and the stirrups from bruising the ankles.

Since the boot's toe was pointed, the foot found the stirrup more easily, while the high heel helped hold it to the stirrup. Being loose on the leg, in the event a cowboy was thrown from his horse, his foot would come out of the boot if it became entangled.

In the final analysis, the cowboy boot was a rider's boot, and definitely "not made for walking!"

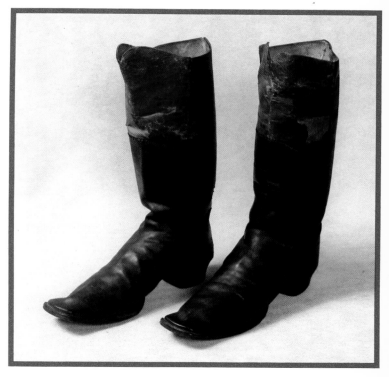

Early square-toed boots, most likely pre-Civil war judging from the construction.

Group of three different, representative cavalry boots of the 1870s. *Don Spaulding.*

Cavalry boots of the 1870s with attached spurs. *Don Spaulding.*

Cavalry boots of the 1870s. *Don Spaulding.*

A pair of Civil War boots that saw many years of service after the war; what is especially interesting is that they are a size 12, huge for those days.

Men and boys' boots from the period 1865 to 1870. Note the quality of construction and the condition after more than 120 years!

Wide-topped boots, especially made in this manner so that pants legs could be stuffed in the tops. *Don Spaulding*.

High-topped boots with mule ear pulls, circa 1880. *Don Spaulding*.

Leather leggings as used by the cavalry instead of boots. These were in vogue from the Civil War, through the Indian Wars, and into the Spanish American War.

Early fringed shotgun chaps with two pockets and a straight waistband, with basket stampings. The straight waistband dates these chaps from the 1870s. At the top is a Colt Model 1860 Army Model revolver converted for cartridges in a "Slim Jim" holster. To the left is an early hand-forged branding iron. *Don Spaulding.*

An excellent pair of unfringed chaps, circa 1870-1880, made by P.A. Monroe, Alva, Oklahoma Territory. Note the flap pockets and the method of fastening down each leg.

Note the repairs to the cuff portion of these shotgun chaps, indicative of hard use. Fringed and with silver conchos down each leg, what makes these chaps unusual are the built-in bullet loops on the belt.

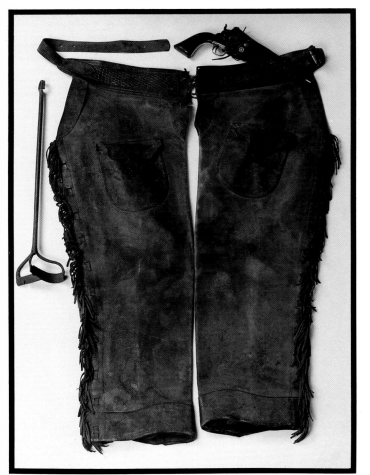

Chaps

Shotgun chaps by R.T. Frazier, Pueblo, Colorado. Highly decorated with silver conchos and fringe down each leg, around the pockets, and on the tooled belt.

The cowboys' chaps are a blend of influences from the past, starting with the vaqueros, who used large leather shields or protectors on their saddles when in heavy brush, saving both horse and rider from the thorny chaparral. As they evolved, chaps became seatless coverings or leggings made of buckskin or other leather, worn to protect the cowhand from rope burns, thorns, abrasions, and the occasional horse bite!

The earlier chaps were climb-in types, where the cowboy had to shuck his boots and spurs. Usually held at the top with a straight belt, they were called "leggings," though they became known as *shot guns* due to the double-barrel appearance of the legs. The search for chaps that were easier to use led to buckles in the back of the leggings, as well as lacing at the front. The cowhand also found that pockets stitched on the legs were a big asset. Fringes down the main seam, as well as silver conchae down the leg, added to the look.

Many cowboys came to prefer the style of chaps known as "batwings," which not only had wrap-around leggings that fastened in back, but were easily snapped on and off. Batwings also gave greater leg protection to the rider and to the horse.

A variation of chaps were the "woollies," used mainly in northern California and the Northwest, where the hides of sheep, goats, or even bear were lined and used for the front of the pants leg, providing warmth, water-shedding qualities, and, not infrequently, a strong odor!

Unnamed shotgun chaps with fringe and silver stud decorations. Note the basket weave on the belt and the fringe around the pockets.

Shotgun chaps with pockets placed on the inside of the chaps rather than the outside as is more the custom.

An unmarked pair of fringed shotgun chaps, with a basket weave tooled belt. Notice the rawhide repair to the cuff area of the right leg.

Finely made Batwing chaps with three large conchos on each leg and heavily studded edges. Note the crossed saber in studs near the bottom of each leg.

These black shotgun chaps are in excellent condition. They do not show a maker's name, but are obviously a quality product. Notice the leaf pattern tooling on the belt area, as well as the heavy conchos and the fringing.

A well-used pair of Batwing chaps made by Stelz Saddlery Co., Houston, Texas. These chaps have four silver conchos down each leg, as well as flap pockets.

A magnificent pair of signed Heiser chaps, with cutout star conchos and lots of nickel spots. They have a laced but dipping belt with three conchos on each side. *Jerard Paul Jordan Galleries/M.L. Gardner Photography.*

Heavily decorated batwing chaps with half moon, Texas star and horse shoe designs run down the outer fringe and carry over onto the belt area, as well as the large silver conchos down each leg. These must have weighed plenty! These chaps came from Chowelah, Washington. *Jerard Paul Jordan Galleries/M.L. Gardner Photography.*

Blood stained Batwing chaps made by the Marfa Saddlery Co., Marfa, Texas.

Chaps by "Cook and Bonney," sporting silver dollar conchos. *Jerard Paul Jordan Galleries/M.L. Gardner Photography.*

Woolly chaps worn by K. E. Stone of the VR Ranch, Glenrock, Wyoming. *Jerard Paul Jordan Galleries/M.L. Gardner Photography.*

Red woolly chaps. *Jerard Paul Jordan Galleries/M.L. Gardner Photography.*

Vaquero Batwing chaps. *Jerard Paul Jordan Galleries/M.L. Gardner Photography.*

Gray angora chaps with heart motif decorations and basket weave tooling on the belt.

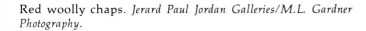

Fringed chaps with pockets, signed "Frank Meanea." *Jerard Paul Jordan Galleries/M.L. Gardner Photography.*

A beautiful pair of black angora chaps.

A good representative example of common, working Batwing chaps with conchos.

Short chaps called "Chinks" worn with high cowboy boots. Shown with a "Running Iron" used to alter existing brands. *Don Spaulding.*

Three different pairs of cowboy cuffs; the left pair shows a pattern of decoration around either end, as well as down the seam, while the middle pair shows a flower pattern in nickel, with nickel rivets at either end. The pair on the right has the omnipresent Star of Texas pointed with nickel rivets. These cuffs are circa 1895.

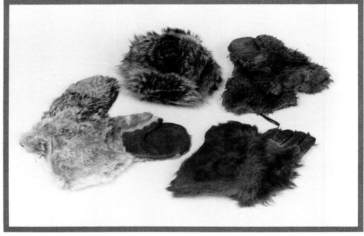

A group of fur gauntlets and a hat, all in excellent original condition. *Don Spaulding.*

Crudely made early cowboy cuffs, with decorations in both German silver and Indian beading. Possibly for Indian use. *Eric Von Schmidt.*

Gauntlets and Cuffs

Picturesque and distinctive looking, gauntlets, or wide cuffed gloves, were worn by practically all cowboys until they were gradually replaced in the 1880s by cuffs and roping gloves. Made by local leather works, the gauntlets and cuffs were quite often highly embossed with floral decorations, Indian heads, steer heads, stars, or other such decorations. Reservation Indians began making both gauntlets and cuffs in the 1880s as a "cottage industry," which has survived to this day. Beaded cuffs and gauntlets, made of fine buckskin, are sought-after collectibles.

Cuffs, which are most often between 6 and 7 inches in length, were made in a number of styles. They can be laced together, snapped, laced and snapped, buckled, buckled and snapped, or buckled and laced. Most often, they were liberally covered with artistic designs. Those bearing a maker's name or cartouche are most highly prized by collectors.

Front and back views of cowboy cuffs, showing the influence of the "Star of Texas." *Don Spaulding*.

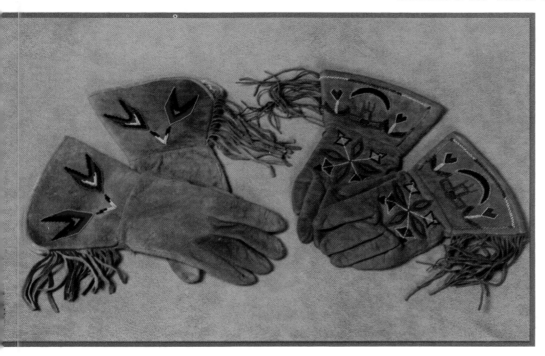

Two pairs of beautifully made, squaw-decorated gloves, as favored by cavalry officers on the plains, circa 1875.

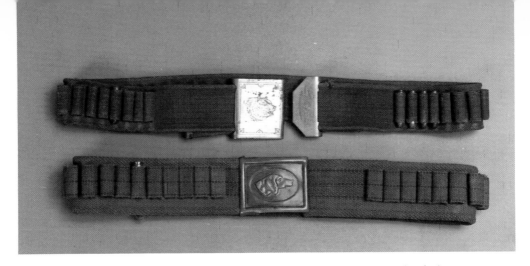

Winchester-made Prairie Belt. Dark tan web cartridge belt in .32 Caliber Winchester. The silvered brass plate has the famous "Bear's Head" design on it's face, while the catch is clearly marked and dated on the face "PAT. FEB 15. 1881/ MANUFACTURED BY THE WINCHESTER REPEATING ARMS CO. / NEW HAVEN, CONN. USA." *Robert Dailey.*

Model 1881 Mills Cartridge belt, .45 caliber with "Dog's Head" buckle. *Robert Dailey.*

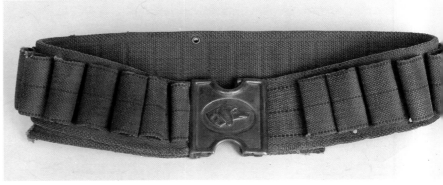

Canvas shotgun belt with Winchester "Dog's Head" buckle. *Don Spaulding.*

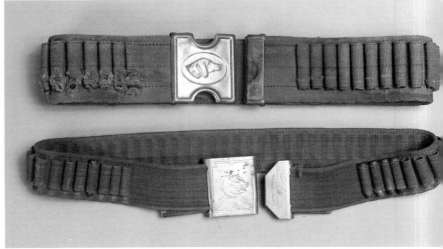

Close detail of both the Winchester "Bear's Head" buckle and the contemporary "Dog's Head" buckle below. *Robert Dailey.*

Another variant of the "Dog's Head" buckle, the "C" buckle, shown above the Winchester "Bear's Head" buckle. *Robert Dailey.*

Belts

The practicality of belts as part of regular attire and for carrying equipment dates from Revolutionary War days. The greatest development came after the Civil War when metallic cartridges, which were carried in loops incorporated in the belts, were introduced. Because a chemical reaction of the brass cartridges with the leather caused verdigris on the cartridges, cartridge loops were frequently made of different textiles.

Different cartridge belts were made for pistol and rifle cartridges, as well as shotgun shells. Shotgun shell belts were usually only a single row of loops, either leather or fabric. Occasionally a belt with riveted metallic shell holders, called "thimbles", will be found.

Rifle and pistol cartridge belts were made with loops in a single row, a double row, or banked one above the other. The fabric loops were sometimes varnished. Due to the cowboys inherent distrust of paper money, combination cartridge and money belts came into vogue, making it possible for specie to be readily carried in the cartridge belt and be easily available.

Types of belts to be found:

The Prairie belt, Model 1876, by Watervliet Arsenal, these were usually a combination of textile and leather.

Quick release cartridge belts, Model 1880, by Mills. The Mills woven cartridge belt was invented by General Anson Mills at Paterson, New Jersey in 1877, with the first loom being built in Worcester, Massachusetts in 1880. That same year the Mills belt became regulation equipment for the U. S. Army. While the Mills Belt Company went out of existence in the 1920s, woven webbing equipment is used worldwide to this day.

Rifle size and revolver size cartridge belts by Winchester. These were most often made of webbing material and incorporated the Winchester logo on the belt buckle

Riding belts (Bronc buster, Kidney belt). The wide bands of the riding belt, with 2 or 3 buckles, act as support for the lower back. These were popular from the early 1900s to approximately 1930.

Beaded squaw belts, These were strictly for show.

Variations included belts with separate tongue and buckle billets, as well as tapered tongues.

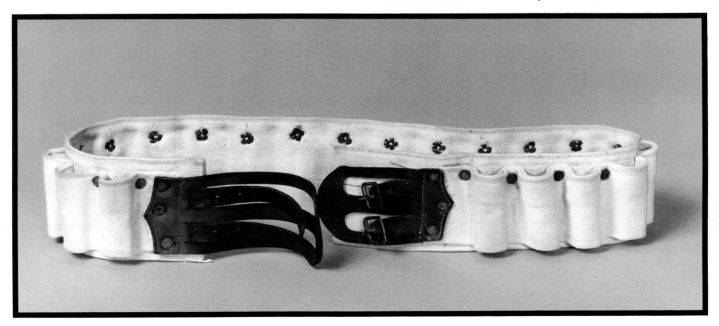

Commercial Shotgun belt. *Robert Dailey.*

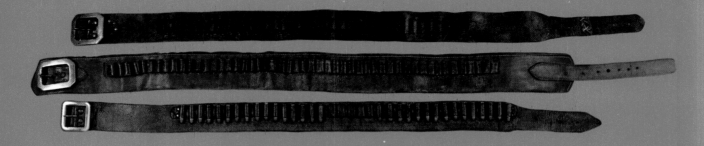

Three pistol cartridge belts, circa 1875 to 1885, all three showing much use. The middle belt is also a money belt. The leather is doubled over to leave space for the bills between the layers.

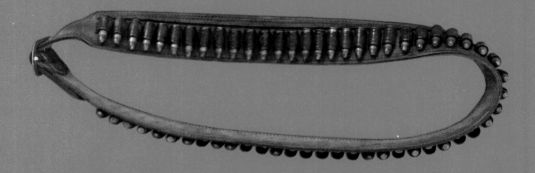

A bandolier loaded with .44 caliber cartridges, absolutely typical of those used on the plains.

(Top) Forager's belt, *Robert Dailey Collection*. (Below) Bandolier of .44 caliber cartridges.

Three canvas Prairie belts, from the top, the 1876 model, the 1879 and the 1881 model. *Don Spaulding*.

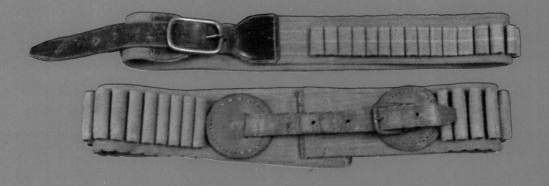

Model 1886 Cavalry Mills Woven Cartridge belt, 45 loops, 45/70 caliber. *Robert Dailey*.

Model 1876 Prairie Style Mills Cartridge belt, with 1879 trial modification. Watervliet Arsenal, A.R. Smith inspector. *Robert Dailey*.

Commercial 12 Gauge Shotgun "Thimble" belt, with metal shell holders attached to the belt. *Robert Dailey.*

Heavily studded bronco busting belt, made to support the back. *Don Spaulding.*

(Top) Double row Military Cartridge belt, circa 1875-1880 (Bottom) Single row Military Cartridge belt, circa 1875-1880. *Jonathan Peck.*

Gun Rigs

Gun rigs, consisting of outfits or sets of belts and holsters, have been used since the development of the pistol. Western gun rigs, used by gunfighters and cowboys, are always associated with the revolver.

Several types of holster rigs were used on the frontier:

The pommel type was hung on the saddle pommel. Colt Walker and Dragoon pistols were carried in this manner.

Military and civilian full-flap style holsters were used for protection of percussion style pistols. The 1851 Navy "belt" pistol was the reason for the design of the military style and pocket revolver holsters. While scarce, these are much easier to find today than the earlier Dragoon model pommel holsters.

The California style, also known as "Slim Jim," had an open top, sewn plug closure, with sewn or riveted belt loops, and a deep cut S-curved top for easy access to the trigger.

The Mexican Loop holster was cut from one piece, with the back slotted to accept the folded-over holster portion, thus eliminating the need for separate belt loops. Buckskin or felt lined, with an "S" curve contour top, this became the standard rig for cowboys. The shorter the holster, the fewer the loops. Those with three loops are highly collectible and most sought after, as are hallmarked pieces. Territorial marked holsters are especially desirable, such as those marked "IT" (Indian Territory), "AT" (Arizona Territory) and "MT" (Montana Territory). Variants of the Mexican Loop holster can be found with riveted loops, while the "Cheyenne" style has a "tear-drop" muzzle plug, ostensibly to keep snow from plugging the muzzle whenever the wearer fell or sat in the snow.

Shoulder holsters were used very early on in the West, going from "full pouch," meaning the pouch that held in the weapon was full-size and uncut, to "skeleton," which was a spring clip shoulder holster in which a leather covered clip clasped the revolver over its cylinder and the muzzle rested in leather "boot" sewn to the bottom of the leather skirt. A later innovation was the "half breed" shoulder holster, which featured a spring-loaded pouch in which the main seam was left open and the revolver could be pulled forward and out with great rapidity.

Belt-mounted clip rigs allowed for a fast draw. For example, the "Bridgeport GI" rig used a slotted metal plate attached to the belt, while a large-headed screw substituted on the frame of the pistol mates with the slot, allowing a rapid draw.

As for the hardware on gun rigs, most early buckles were cast brass or bronze and unplated. Early rigs will display snaps and tubular rivets, as well as copper washer style rivets, the latter continuing in use to the present day.

A really beautiful and rare belt rig of holster, knife, and sheath. The simple belt strap indicates pre-cartridge use. Circa 1860. *Don Spaulding.*

Pommel bag holsters, signed Main and Winchester, San Francisco, California. Post-Civil War period. Very fine condition. *Jerard Paul Jordan Galleries/M.L. Gardner Photography.*

(Left) Tooled "Mexican Loop" holster. (Right) Military saddle holsters, circa 1850. Belonged to General Noble, who fought in the Mexican War.

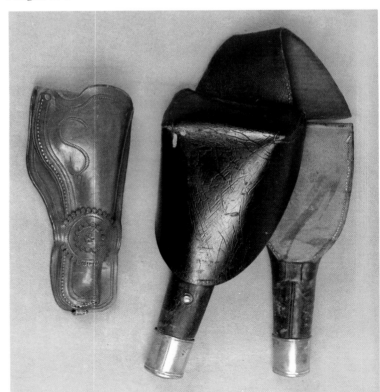

Early double pommel holster. Signed in script, "S. F., CA. 1854." *Jerard Paul Jordan Galleries/M.L. Gardner Photography.*

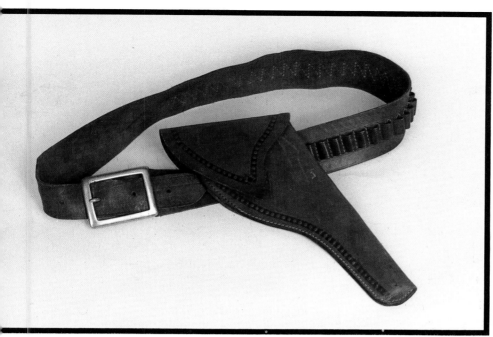

Civilian-style gun rig, the holster with a button down flap.
Don Spaulding.

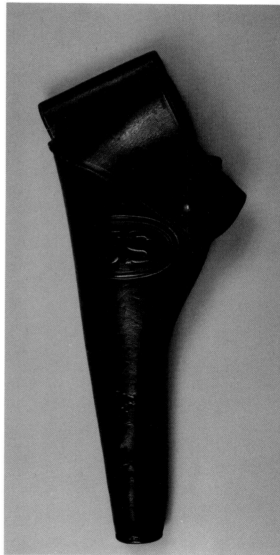

U.S. marked Single Action Colt holster
in mint condition. *Larry Kaufman.*

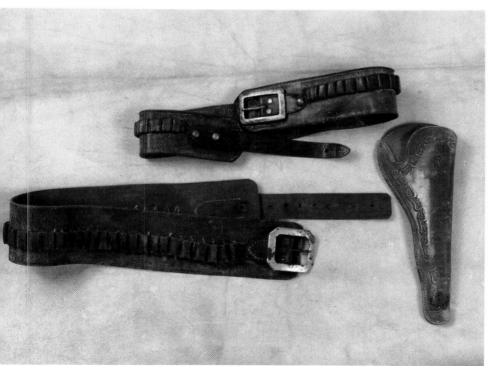

Group showing "Slim Jim" California style holster, with a
pistol belt and a rifle belt. *Jonathan Peck.*

Two "Slim Jim" holsters flanking a beautiful Indian-beaded holster. *Don Spaulding*.

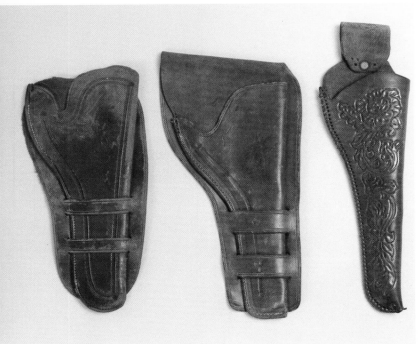

Two Mexican double loop holsters on the left, with a "Slim Jim" holster on the right.

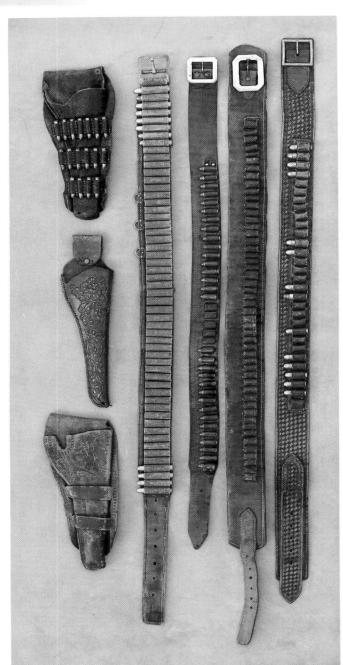

A grouping of three holsters and four cartridge belts, circa 1875-1880. Three different styles of holsters are shown. The top holster is unusual in that stitched cartridge loops are part of the holster, the second is an excellent example of the "Slim Jim," and at the bottom is a two loop Mexican style holster. Of the cartridge belts, the first belt from the left is the model 1876 cartridge belt with the 1879 three brass ring modification. The next three belts are all representative of those found in the West; the middle belt is also a money belt.

Unmarked Mexican loop holster and gun belt, typical of those found in the West. *Don Spaulding.*

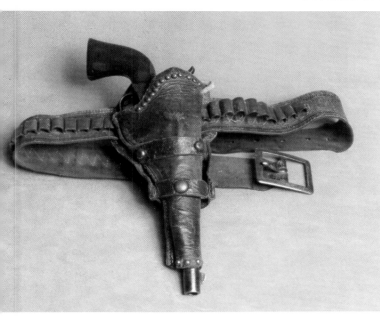

Studded double loop "Mexican Loop" holster with Colt Single Action revolver in the holster. *Steve Crowley.*

Laced Mexican loop holster and belt; notice the wide backing to the holster. *Don Spaulding.*

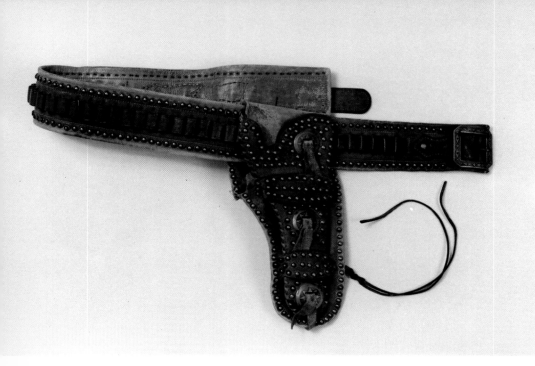

Highly decorated belt and holster, Pueblo, Colorado.
Jonathan Peck.

Colt Single Action .45 caliber revolver, ivory grips with carved eagle's head. Floral tooled belt and holster, with silver eagle and silver star. The star is marked "C.R.C. 20." *Eric von Schmidt/Ed Vebell.*

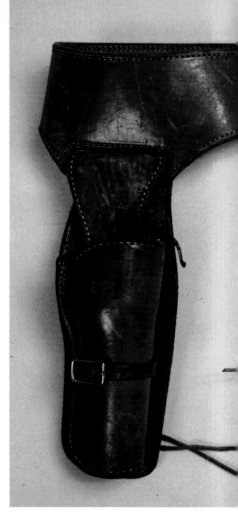

Buscadero-style gunfighter's rig with tie-down thongs.

These well-used working cowboy's holsters are typical of the West. The holster on the left is for a long barrel revolver, with a deep cutout for the trigger guard and simply stitched. The middle piece is most likely homemade with thong stitching. The right holster shows an overly large back flap and a double loop construction, with loops generously decorated, as well as a deep medallion on the upper front. The first two holsters are circa 1875-1880, while the right piece is circa 1890, with none of them being marked.

Holster with money and cartridge belt, signed R. T. Frazier, Pueblo, Colorado, circa 1900. Both the money-cartridge belt and holster are signed, and both incorporate an outstanding tooled floral pattern. Mint condition with the exception of the final six inches of the belt tongue. A truly outstanding and rare piece. *Jerard Paul Jordan Galleries/M.L. Gardner Photography.*

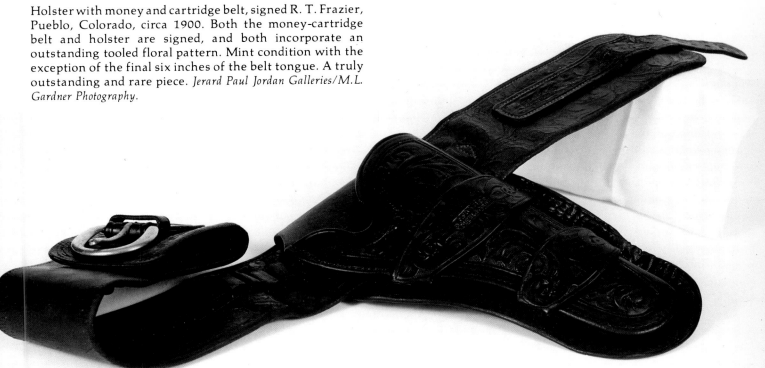

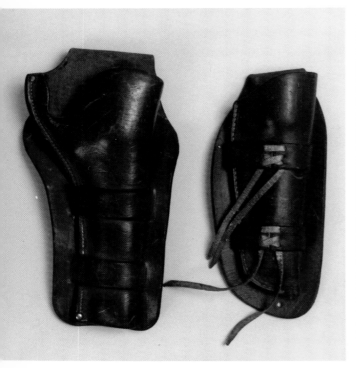

(Left) Mexican loop holster made by Herman H. Heiser Co., Denver, Colorado. (Right) Late gunfighter-style holster.

Gun rig of belt with bullets and a single loop holster. *Don Spaulding.*

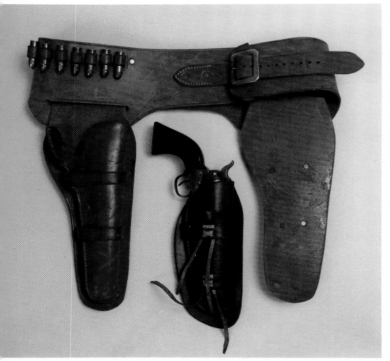

"Double Rig" Buscadero-style gun belt and holsters with Colt Single Action revolver in it's original holster.

Very well made and unmarked Mexican loop holster and gun belt with bullets. *Don Spaulding.*

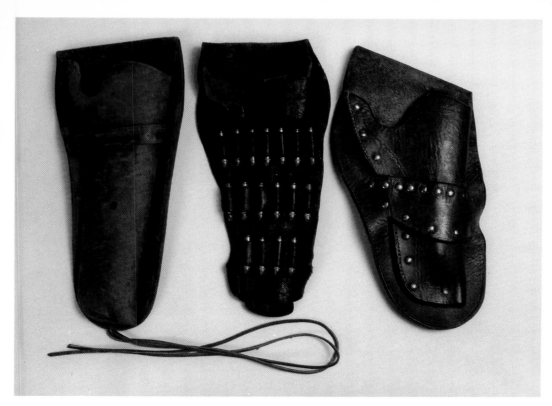

The single loop holster to the left is for a long barrel pistol, with the single loop riveted to the holster and the tie-down thong attached. The middle holster is unusual in that there is provision for 17 cartridges in the loops attached to the outside of the holster; note how the upper edge of the holster has been cut away at some time in the past to accommodate a different style of pistol. The holster on the right shows a well-used single loop style, well-decorated with nickel plated rivets and showing a generous back flap. All pieces are unmarked and are circa 1880.

Three Mexican loop holsters, circa 1885. On the left is a well-decorated and well-used double loop holster; the middle holster is an example of the single loop with a ring for tie-down thongs and is in excellent condition. The holster on the right, though well-used, is another fine specimen of the double loop holster, with a deep cutout for the trigger guard. These are all unmarked pieces.

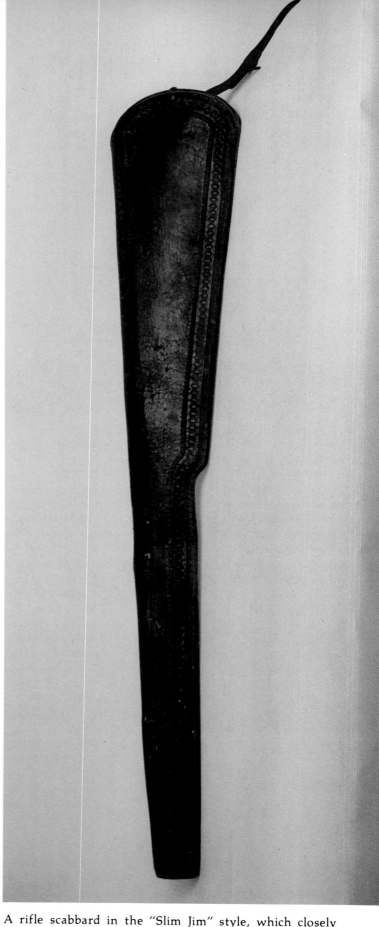

Rawhide laced Mexican loop holster, sporting two loops. *Don Spaulding.*

A rifle scabbard in the "Slim Jim" style, which closely follows the contours of the rifle. *Don Spaulding.*

Pistols

While his were not the only pistols to be found in the West, the name Samuel Colt was synonymous with the pistol found strapped to the waist of almost every cowboy on the frontier. The earliest Colt revolver, produced in 1836, was known as the Paterson Colt, because it was developed at the facility in Paterson, New Jersey. This pistol introduced nearly every basic construction feature that was to be used during the next twenty years. Those features included the placement of the cap cones at the rear of the loading chamber, fence separation of the cones to cut down on chain ignition, mechanical locking of the cylinder at the moment of firing so that the cylinder chamber and the bore of the barrel were properly aligned, and the rotation of the cylinder by the cocking of the hammer.

The Paterson Colts were designed in a variety of calibers and barrel lengths, with the smallest, the "Baby Paterson," having a 2½" barrel. One Paterson model had interchangeable barrels of 4½" and 12". The most popular of these Patersons was the "Texas Paterson," a belt model in .40 caliber with a 7½" barrel.

In 1846, Captain Sam Walker of the Texas Rangers, an old friend of Sam Colt, persuaded President Polk and his Secretary of War to give Colt an order for 1,000 pistols. These pistols, manufactured in 1847 in conjunction with Eli Whitney in Whitneyville, Connecticut, were known as the "Walker Colt." They were six-shot, single action. 44 caliber pistols weighing 4 pounds, 9 ounces...a staggering handful!

In 1848, Hartford, Connecticut became the location for Colt's manufacturing operation, and one of the first pistols produced there was the Model 1848, a .44 caliber six-shot, single action Dragoon. There were three different versions of the Dragoon model. The first had a loading lever with latch projecting from the front end, while the second version, produced in 1850, had rectangular slots cut in the cylinder, with some pieces having an oval trigger guard as opposed to the usual square-back trigger guard common to the Dragoons. The third version had a butt designed for use with a detachable shoulder stock. All three were issued to mounted troops, i. e., Dragoons.

Some of the finest percussion revolvers were made by Remington. The first model was a .36 caliber six-shot, fluted cylinder, 6½" octagon barreled revolver produced for the Navy. The most popular Civil War model was the Remington .44 caliber six-shot, 8" barrel revolver, that weighed in at 2 pounds, 14 ounces.

Remingtons were constructed with a solid frame, and top strap and grip straps integral with the frame. Pistols made by Pettingill, Freeman, Rogers and Spencer, Savage-North, Starr, and Whitney all followed the solid frame construction. Conversely, Colt, Cooper, Manhattan, Metropolitan, and Walch employed an open frame construction that was less rigid. Colt eventually changed over to the solid frame construction with his cartridge pistols.

Besides Colt and Remington, Eben T. Starr was responsible for some of the finest Civil War weapons. The most popular was a .44 caliber double action revolver, closely followed by a six-shot, single action .36 caliber revolver that was lighter and smaller.

(Top) Colt pocket pistol, showing it's holster below it. On the bottom is a lady's suede holster for a small pistol to be carried in a handbag.

In 1857, Smith and Wesson started production on America's first metal cartridge revolver. As Colt was the leader in the percussion revolver field until 1869, Smith and Wesson, due to patent rights, retained a virtual monopoly in the metallic cartridge field. In that year, the Model 1869 "American" was introduced, a six-shot, single action .44 caliber revolver. It was followed by the S & W model of 1875, a .45 caliber six-shot single action revolver. In the West the S & W sheathed trigger six-shot .32 was a leading contender of the day.

Not to be outdone, Colt then made a strong comeback in the revolver field. The Model 1873 Colt still was the favorite of western gunmen. Originally introduced as a six-shot .45 caliber, it was re-chambered to take a Henry .44 or Winchester .44-40. This caliber cartridge was well received in the West in that cartridges for the Winchester rifle were made interchangeable with the Colt '73 pistol. The pistol was so popular it remained in production until 1941.

The single action six-shooter of 1873 is uncontested as the most popular revolver ever made. It has been referred to as the "Peacemaker," "Equalizer," "Hogleg," "The Six Gun," and "Frontier Model." Solidly constructed and weighing only 2½ pounds, the Single Action Army, as it is also called, offered a limitless number of variations in addition to the caliber options. There were U. S. martially marked pieces, target pieces, Bisley and Bisley target pieces, the Sheriff's Model, the Buntline Special, and a variety of odd barrel lengths.

Sheriff Pat Garrett of New Mexico brought the career of William Bonney, otherwise known as "Billy The Kid" to an abrupt halt with his .44 caliber single action Colt...the same model pistol The Kid used to make a record of at least 21 killings! Sheriff Bat Masterson of Ford County, Kansas felt undressed without his Peacemaker, while Wyatt Earp of Dodge City never left home without his Frontier model. This is the model pistol that most often comes to mind whenever the question arises as to which handgun ruled the West!

1875 was a big year for other pistol manufacturers as well, with firms such as Merwin Hulbert and Co., Hopkins and Allen, and Forehand and Wadsworth making martial weapons and heavy-duty western-style pistols. While a collector will undoubtedly find other makes of pistols, the ones mentioned had the biggest impact during the cowboy's Western heyday.

An excellent example of an Eli Whitney Civil War era, navy-style .36 caliber six shot revolver, with 7 3/16" octagon barrel and walnut grips. Serial number 17759. On the cylinder is a maritime scene with shield showing the Whitneyville plant. This particular series of pistols was made at the Whitney Armory during the administration of Eli Whitney Jr. who came of age in November, 1842. He carried on the business that had been administered by a board of trustees since his father's death. *Museum of Connecticut History.*

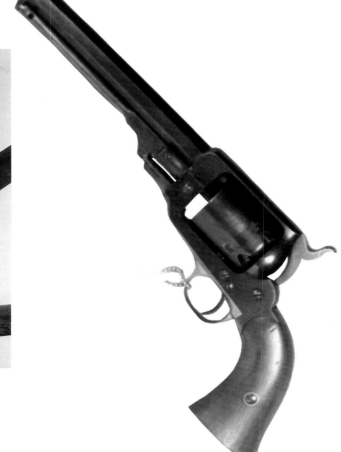

On the hub, a Colt Model 1877 "Lightning" Double Action revolver, while a Colt Model 1862 Police revolver rests against the spoke.

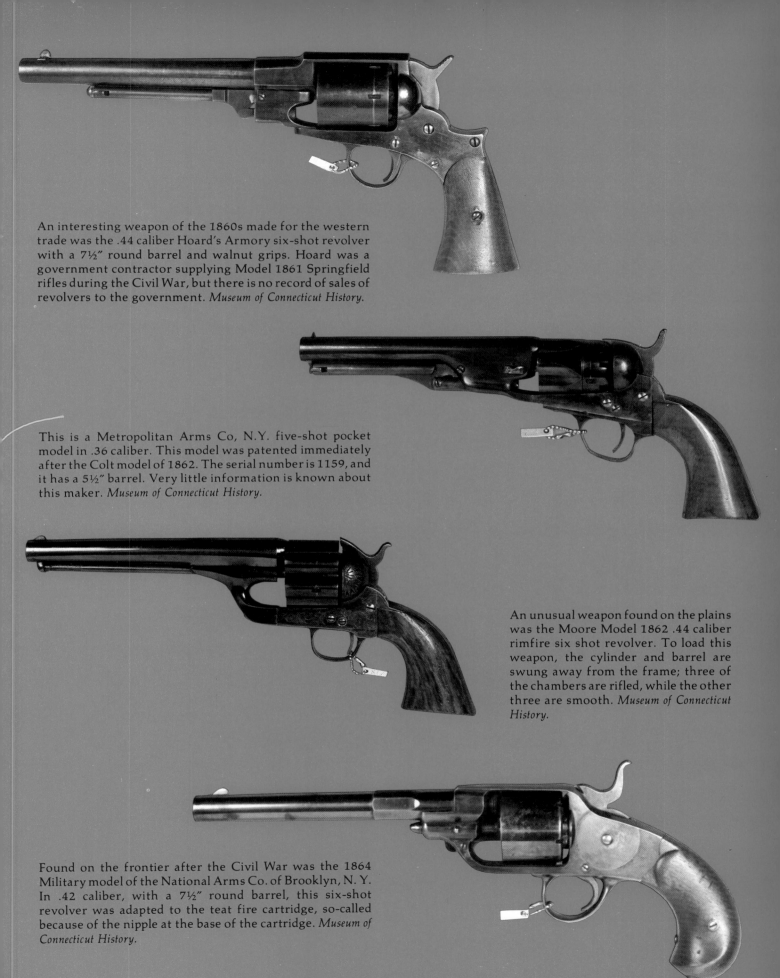

An interesting weapon of the 1860s made for the western trade was the .44 caliber Hoard's Armory six-shot revolver with a 7½" round barrel and walnut grips. Hoard was a government contractor supplying Model 1861 Springfield rifles during the Civil War, but there is no record of sales of revolvers to the government. *Museum of Connecticut History.*

This is a Metropolitan Arms Co, N.Y. five-shot pocket model in .36 caliber. This model was patented immediately after the Colt model of 1862. The serial number is 1159, and it has a 5½" barrel. Very little information is known about this maker. *Museum of Connecticut History.*

An unusual weapon found on the plains was the Moore Model 1862 .44 caliber rimfire six shot revolver. To load this weapon, the cylinder and barrel are swung away from the frame; three of the chambers are rifled, while the other three are smooth. *Museum of Connecticut History.*

Found on the frontier after the Civil War was the 1864 Military model of the National Arms Co. of Brooklyn, N. Y. In .42 caliber, with a 7½" round barrel, this six-shot revolver was adapted to the teat fire cartridge, so-called because of the nipple at the base of the cartridge. *Museum of Connecticut History.*

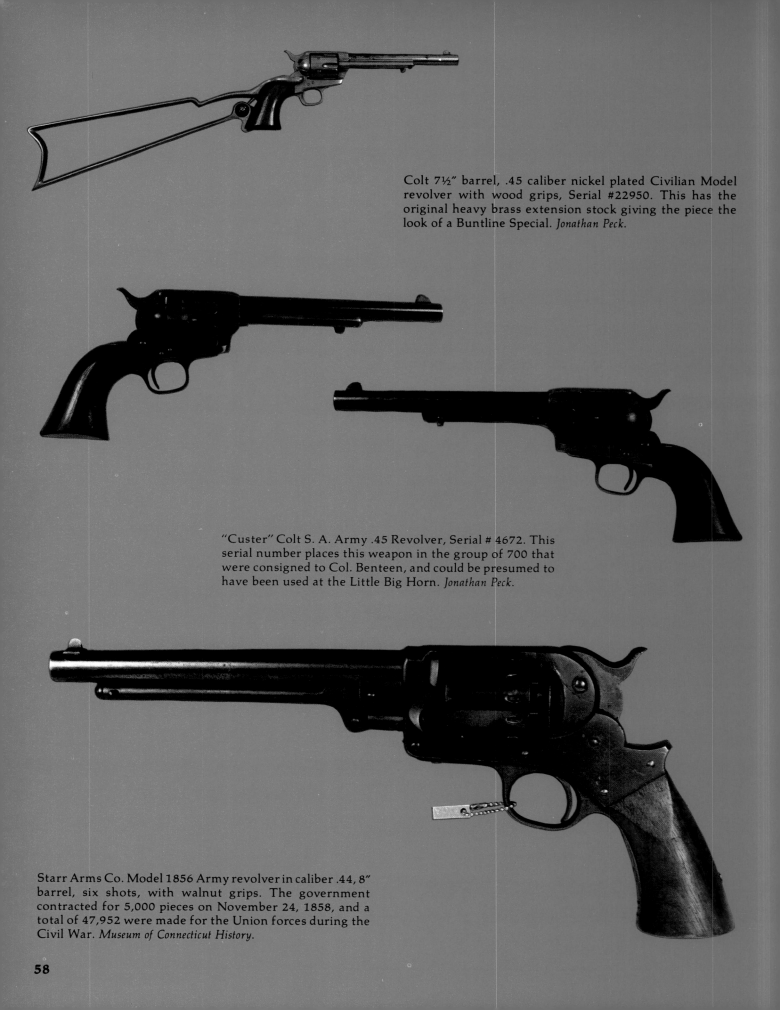

Colt 7½" barrel, .45 caliber nickel plated Civilian Model revolver with wood grips, Serial #22950. This has the original heavy brass extension stock giving the piece the look of a Buntline Special. *Jonathan Peck.*

"Custer" Colt S. A. Army .45 Revolver, Serial # 4672. This serial number places this weapon in the group of 700 that were consigned to Col. Benteen, and could be presumed to have been used at the Little Big Horn. *Jonathan Peck.*

Starr Arms Co. Model 1856 Army revolver in caliber .44, 8" barrel, six shots, with walnut grips. The government contracted for 5,000 pieces on November 24, 1858, and a total of 47,952 were made for the Union forces during the Civil War. *Museum of Connecticut History.*

Colt Single Action Army revolver, with a 7½" barrel. Note the "Eagle and Shield" pattern on the hard rubber grips.

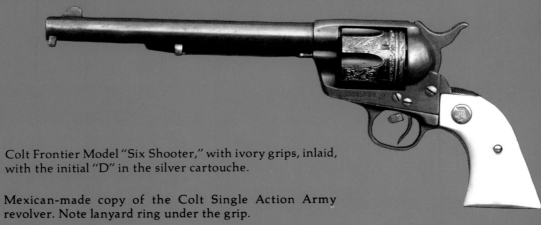

Colt Frontier Model "Six Shooter," with ivory grips, inlaid, with the initial "D" in the silver cartouche.

Mexican-made copy of the Colt Single Action Army revolver. Note lanyard ring under the grip.

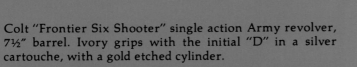

Colt "Frontier Six Shooter" single action Army revolver, 7½" barrel. Ivory grips with the initial "D" in a silver cartouche, with a gold etched cylinder.

Colt 5½" barrel .45 caliber revolver, serial # 343242. Silver with gold plated cylinder and double carved Steer Head Ivory grips with sunken medallions. Presented to E. A. Brininstool, author of many Custer articles. *Jonathan Peck.*

Backstrap detail of E.A. Brininstool presentation piece. *Jonathan Peck.*

Colt Single Action Army revolver, Artillery model "Peacemaker" with its serial number in the 7,000 range, denoting possible use by Custer's men.

A beautiful pair of Colt 7½" barrel, .45 caliber revolvers, nickel plated with ivory handles, in their own fitted case with ammunition. Engraving by Gustav Young. *Jonathan Peck.*

Colt 4¾", .45 caliber revolver, nickel plated with pearl grips; engraved by Cuno Helfricht. Shipped to Shapeleigh Hardware, St. Louis, Missouri, in May, 1899. Engraved on backstrap "W.B. Jackson Gray Horse, I.T." Mr. Jackson was the sheriff on the Indian Reservation of Gray Horse, Indian Territory. This is now known as Fairfax, Oklahoma. This is a rare and very difficult to find original sheriff's presentation piece; letter on file shows the piece was shipped to Shapeleigh Hardware and sold to Jackson. *Jonathan Peck.*

Grouping of items belonging to Sheriff Jackson, including his picture, original badge, handcuffs, and a lock from the Fairfax jail. *Jonathan Peck.*

Close up of the engraving on the backstrap of the Jackson presentation pistol. *Jonathan Peck.*

Colt Sheriff's Model S.A. .45 Revolver. *Jonathan Peck.*

Colt 7½" .45 caliber revolver, full blued, with carved ivory grips, serial # 304972. One of two shipped to a New York agency in 1908. *Jonathan Peck.*

Colt 7½" barrel, .45 caliber revolver. Silvered with pearl grips, Serial # 318380. Engraved by Cuno Helfricht and shipped to Chicago in 1911. *Jonathan Peck.*

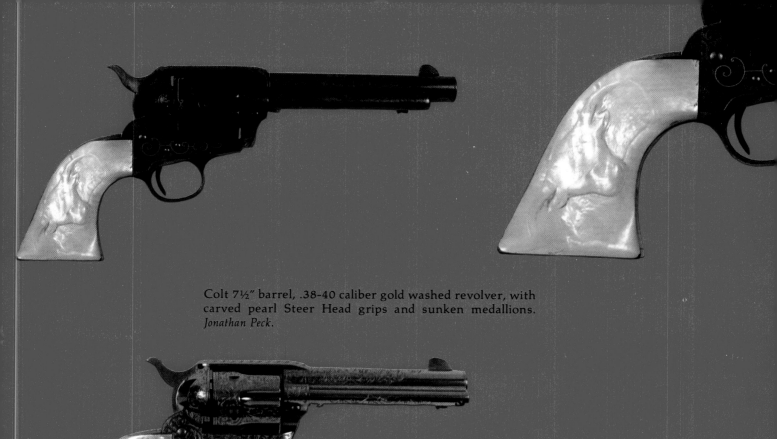

Colt 7½" barrel, .38-40 caliber gold washed revolver, with carved pearl Steer Head grips and sunken medallions. *Jonathan Peck.*

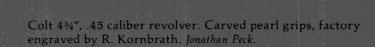

Colt 4¾", .45 caliber revolver. Carved pearl grips, factory engraved by R. Kornbrath. *Jonathan Peck.*

Colt .45 caliber 7½" barrel, nickel-and gold-washed. Engraved by L. D. Nimschke, shipped to H & D Folsom, N.Y.C., with back strap so marked; used by them as a demonstrator. In the 32xxx serial range. Circa 1876. *Jonathan Peck.*

A reliable performer in the West was the Remington 1858 New Model Army Conversion, .46 caliber rimfire five-shot revolver with an 8" octagonal barrel. Serial number 48. *Museum of Connecticut History*.

Original Smith and Wesson advertising poster for their revolvers. Found by the author in a Cape Cod gunshop.

Remington New Model Army revolver. This was the chief competitor to the Colt 1860 Army revolver during the Civil War.

An updated Remington was the Army model 1875 Single Action six shot revolver in .44 caliber. 7½" round barrel with walnut grips. *Museum of Connecticut History.*

A standby for the military as well as for civilians was the Smith and Wesson .44 caliber, center fire six-shot revolver, as adopted by the army for use by the cavalry. Incidently, the Russian government purchased 20,000 of these revolvers for their cavalry. *Museum of Connecticut History.*

A grouping of three pocket model pistols, including a Remington pocket model .22 caliber single shot, with a 3¼" round barrel with walnut grips. Next is a Remington 1st model .31 caliber five-shot revolver, serial number 15, with a 31/16" octagon barrel. The last piece is a Forehand and Wadsworth pocket, double action, five-shot .38 caliber rimfire revolver, with a 3" barrel and birdshead walnut grips. Pistols such as these could be readily concealed and played their part in the history of the West. *Museum of Connecticut History.*

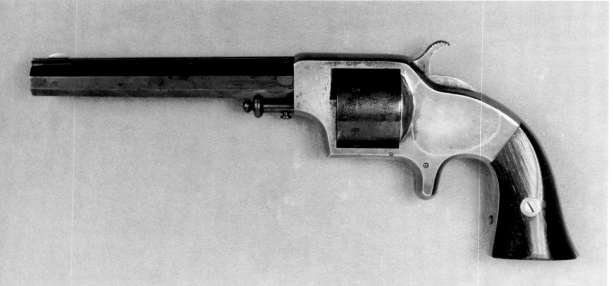

Plant Manufacturing Co. of New Haven, Connecticut produced this third model "Army" revolver with a 6" octagonal barrel. *Museum of Connecticut History.*

A second group of "hide-away" pocket pistols includes a nice example of a F.A. Hood Co., .38 caliber, five-shot, pocket pistol, with a 2½" round barrel and birdshead butt with walnut grips. The second piece is an Eli Whitney .38 caliber single action, five-shot pocket pistol, again with a birdshead butt and walnut grips. It has a 2" octagonal barrel, serial number 15. Lastly is a Remington .41 caliber double barrel derringer pocket pistol, with 3" barrel, birdshead butt and rubber grips. These three qualify as excellent back-up weapons. *Museum of Connecticut History.*

A fine example of the Remington Model 1875 Single Action Army revolver, nickel-plated and with the lanyard ring missing. This piece was purchased in Mexico City in 1950 for $18.00!

Color print of "Tex and Patches" for Colt Firearms by Frank Schoonover. *Museum of Connecticut History.*

A tribute to the past! Here we have the commemorative model of "Gunfighters of the Old West," and the commemorative model of "Outlaws of the Old West." A fine modern payment of respect to history. *Museum of Connecticut History.*

FIGHTING TO SAVE THEIR HIDES
by Don Spaulding, S.A.H.A.

"Fighting to Save the Horses," by Don Spaulding.
Meticulously researched and recreated with models
wearing original clothing and using original horse gear. Oil
on gesso panel.

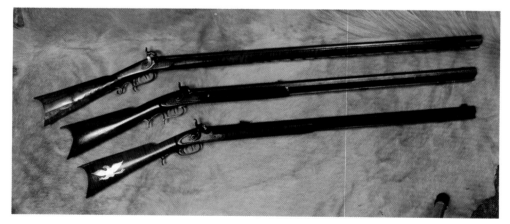

Early type rifles still found on the frontier after the Civil
War. They are, from the top:

1. H. Elwell warranted back lock, tiger striped full stock
with brass decorative patch box. 2. Plains rifle with
heavy octagonal barrel; half stocked. Barrel is inscribed
"I. Sheets, Nov. the 25th, 1863 Ohio." 3. Half stocked
Plains rifle with octagonal barrel and silver eagle inlay.

Rifles

While many percussion type rifles were being used on the frontier at the end of the Civil War, this section will focus on cartridge rifles, both single shot as well as magazine fed. When one thinks of rifles carried by cowboys and frontiersmen, names like Sharps, Springfield, Henry, Winchester, Evans, Remington, Colt, and Spencer are those that immediately come to mind. While weapons made by others will certainly be found, the foregoing are the contenders for most popular rifle in the West, with honors going to Winchester.

One of the most famous repeating rifles was the Spencer, developed during the Civil War. Originally made in .52 caliber, this model was a seven-shot, lever action weapon weighing approximately ten pounds. It was operated by a hand lever beneath the trigger, which acted as a trigger guard. The arm is loaded through a tube in the butt plate, with cartridges lined up, one in front of the other. Over 12, 000 Spencer Carbines were purchased by the government during the Civil War, and many ended up on the frontier when the war was over.

The old time buffalo hunters favored the Sharps rifle for bringing down their prey. Originally a percussion piece, those produced after the Civil War utilized practically all of the parts of the older vertical block percussion model, except for the substitution of a new block incorporating a firing pin, modification of the hammer, and the addition of an extractor. The introduction in 1877 of the radically different Borchardt model necessitated the end of the use of percussion parts. The metallic cartridge side hammer Sharps was one of the most rugged and popular breech-loaders of its time, being extremely simple to clean and easy to repair, thus making it a favorite with buffalo hunters of the day.

The Springfield Trap Door Carbine Model 1870 in caliber .45-70 was found in quantity in the West, as it was the official Army issue of the day. The decision to equip troops with a single shot weapon was inexplicable, considering that from the Civil War on the American civilian—the cattleman, the law officer, the market hunter, and the outlaw, as well as a few fortunate Indians—had all the firepower they needed with their repeating rifles.

The repeating rifles that had the greatest impact on the West were the Henry and its descendants, the

(Left) The Spencer model 1865 .52 caliber rimfire carbine served at the end of the Civil War and well into the Indian wars. It is commonly referred to as the "Indian Model." Note the walnut stock and forearm, the lever action breech and side hammer. (Right) Of interest to the collector is the .50 caliber center fire carbine made by A.H. Rowe of Hartford, Connecticut in 1864. This particular weapon is serial number 3! This hammerless carbine has two triggers, one for cocking and one for firing. Releasing the tang latch allows the barrel and receiver to tip out to the right for loading. *Museum of Connecticut History.*

Winchesters. The Henry was named after B. Tyler Henry, plant superintendent at Winchester. He developed a lever action rifle that manually cocked the hammer, ejected the shell, and fed a cartridge into the chamber. The cartridges developed by Henry improved on the original Smith and Wesson patents for the expandable metallic case and were as important as the rifle itself. This repeater carried fifteen .44 caliber cartridges in a tubular magazine under the barrel. While the Henry presented no serious competition to the Spencer during the Civil War, after the war the Spencer was overshadowed by the Henry's successor—the Winchester Model 1866.

The '66 was essentially a Henry with side gate loading, called "King's Improvement." This eliminated the problem of dirt clogging the magazine feed tube, as often happened with the Henry. With the Model 1866, the Winchester Repeating Firearms Company finally hit pay dirt. The Model 1866 was so popular that it remained in the product line until 1898. The "Yellow Boy," as it was known because of it's brass receiver, was in appearance and mechanism one of the finest Winchesters ever made.

Following the 1866 model came the famous Model 1873; this was produced as a successor to the Model 1866 only because of the improvements it featured, having a stronger action and chambering more powerful centerfire cartridges. This was truly considered "The Gun That Won The West." With it, Winchester, for the first time, offered an array of custom order features. In addition to the standard carbine, rifle, and musket configurations, a customer could order a special barrel length, half-round or half-octagon barrel, special heavy weight barrel, or special magazine, custom engravings, set triggers and the now famous "1 of 1, 000" and "1 of 100" select barrel series.

At the request of big game hunters as well as shooters, the Model 1873 was followed by the Model 1876, basically a large caliber version of the Model 1873. Since it was presented at the Philadelphia Centennial of 1876, the name "Centennial Model" was soon adopted.

The next lever action model to emerge was the 1886 Model, chambered for express cartridges and capable of handling loads that were too much for the '76. This new model was such a vast improvement that it immediately affected sales of the '76. Produced in over a dozen different calibers, as well as innumerable styles, the Model '86 became an immediate favorite of Teddy Roosevelt, who quickly replaced his '76 with a deluxe .45-90 rifle.

The next evolution in the lever action Winchester was the Model 1892, which was simply a scaled-down version of the 1886, firing the .44-40, .38-40, and .32-20 cartridges. Once again, custom order selections allowed a great variety of barrel lengths, magazine sizes, and other features at extra cost. There are probably more of these carbines and rifles still in use today than there are in collections.

Made for smokeless powder cartridges, the Model 1894 Winchester rifle and carbine are still in production at this time. The last Winchester from this period was the box magazine Model 1895 lever action, made in carbine, rifle and musket styles. Historically, the '95 was a popular service weapon during the Spanish American War and another favorite of Teddy Roosevelt.

The silver eagle inlay on the half-stock Plains rifle.

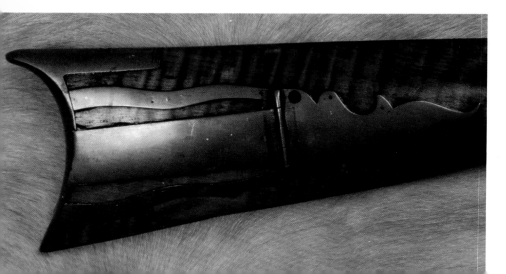

Close up of the detail of the brass patch box on the H. Elwell back lock rifle.

Detail on the barrel of the I. Sheets, Ohio Plains rifle.

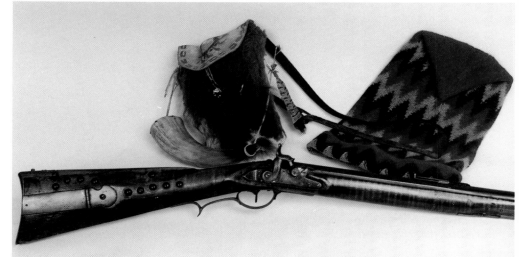

An early hunting bag, stocking cap, and a beautiful trade rifle, marked "J. Henry" and including "U.S." stampings. *Don Spaulding.*

Produced in Providence, Rhode Island, the Model 1856, .54 caliber Burnside percussion carbine performed equally well in peace and in war. This specimen is in factory new condition. *Museum of Connecticut History.*

Close-up of the markings on the "Henry" trade rifle. Rifles marked "U.S." were for trade with the Indians. *Don Spaulding.*

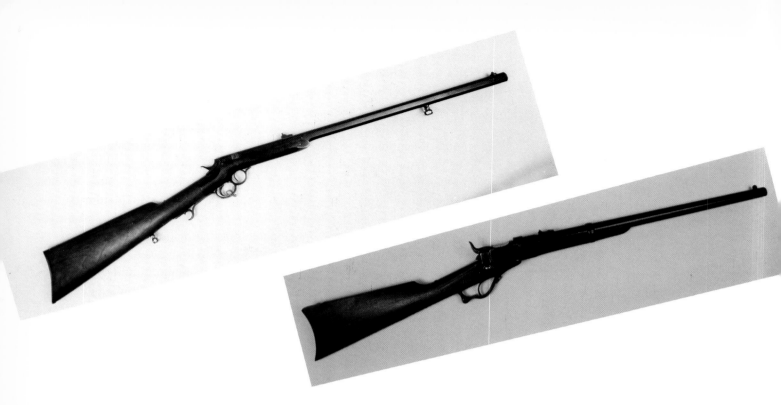

In excellent condition, this Massachusetts Arms Co. Model 1854 .44 caliber is an early 1st model percussion carbine. This particular specimen does not carry a serial number. Note the double set triggers and the leaf sight. *Museum of Connecticut History.*

One of the early workhorses on the plains was the Starr .54 caliber, side-hammer, lever action, percussion carbine. This piece, serial number 39951, is in mint condition. During the Civil War, 20,601 of this model carbine were delivered to the government. *Museum of Connecticut History.*

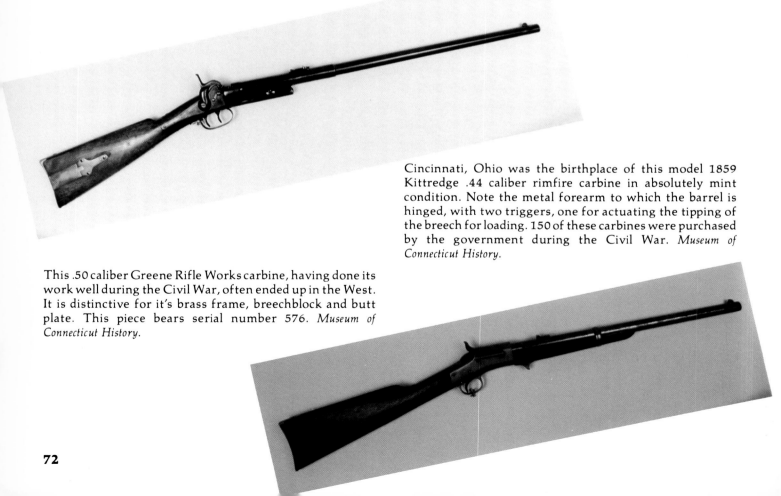

Cincinnati, Ohio was the birthplace of this model 1859 Kittredge .44 caliber rimfire carbine in absolutely mint condition. Note the metal forearm to which the barrel is hinged, with two triggers, one for actuating the tipping of the breech for loading. 150 of these carbines were purchased by the government during the Civil War. *Museum of Connecticut History.*

This .50 caliber Greene Rifle Works carbine, having done its work well during the Civil War, often ended up in the West. It is distinctive for it's brass frame, breechblock and butt plate. This piece bears serial number 576. *Museum of Connecticut History.*

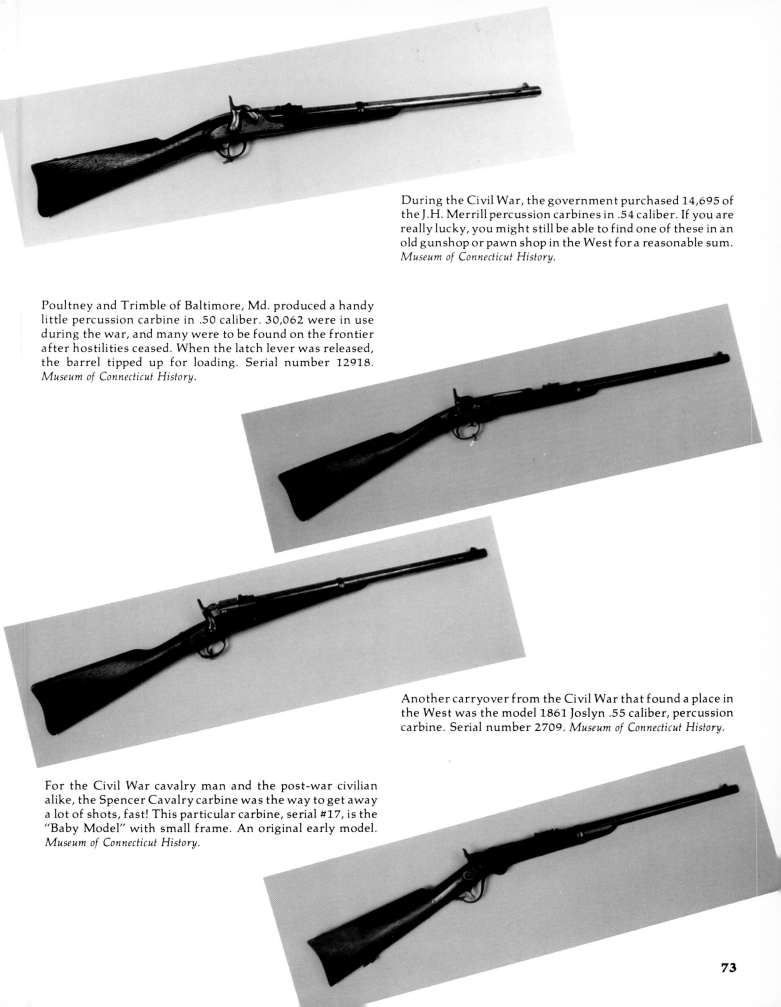

During the Civil War, the government purchased 14,695 of the J.H. Merrill percussion carbines in .54 caliber. If you are really lucky, you might still be able to find one of these in an old gunshop or pawn shop in the West for a reasonable sum. *Museum of Connecticut History.*

Poultney and Trimble of Baltimore, Md. produced a handy little percussion carbine in .50 caliber. 30,062 were in use during the war, and many were to be found on the frontier after hostilities ceased. When the latch lever was released, the barrel tipped up for loading. Serial number 12918. *Museum of Connecticut History.*

Another carryover from the Civil War that found a place in the West was the model 1861 Joslyn .55 caliber, percussion carbine. Serial number 2709. *Museum of Connecticut History.*

For the Civil War cavalry man and the post-war civilian alike, the Spencer Cavalry carbine was the way to get away a lot of shots, fast! This particular carbine, serial #17, is the "Baby Model" with small frame. An original early model. *Museum of Connecticut History.*

Not often found is the E.G. Lamson and Son carbine in .50 caliber centerfire. Although the government purchased 1,000 of this model, this particular weapon does not bear a serial number. *Museum of Connecticut History.*

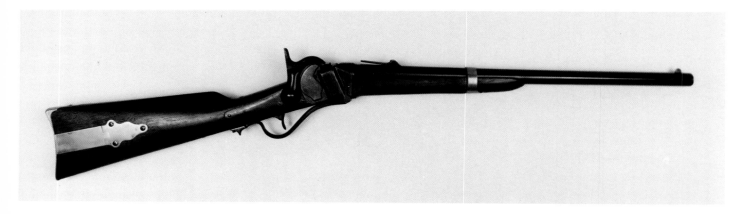

One of the better known weapons in the west was the Slant Breech Sharp's carbine, a product of Hartford, Connecticut. In .52 caliber, this model 1855 side-hammer arm with it's brass butt plate, patch box and barrel bands was quite distinctive. It proved it's worth in war and peace. Serial number 17331. *Museum of Connecticut History.*

(Top) The Sharps Model 1859 carbine converted to metallic cartridge in 1867. (Bottom) Sharps Model 1874 rifle, .45 caliber "Old Reliable." Bridgeport, Conn.

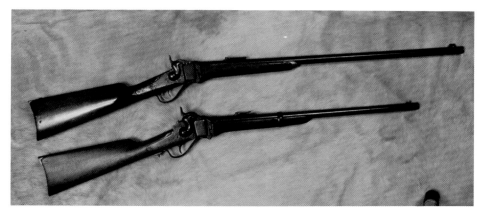

(Top) Sharps rifle, (Old Reliable), .45 caliber, serial #C33376
(Bottom) Sharps Carbine, post-Civil War conversion.

The "Old Reliable" stamping on the barrel of the Sharps
rifle.

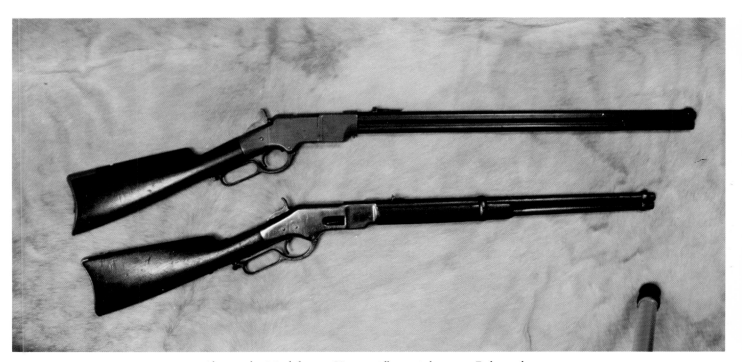

Above, the Model 1860 Henry rifle, serial #1705. Below, the
famous "Yellow Boy" Winchester 1866 saddle ring carbine,
so called because of the brass receiver. Serial # 39711.

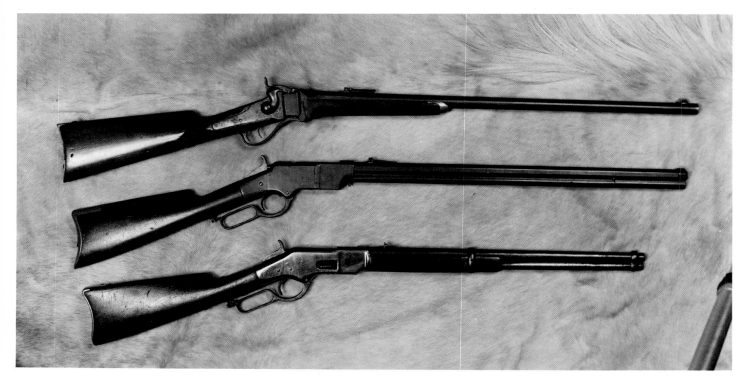

Three standbys in the West, from the top:

1. Sharps rifle (Old Reliable), 1869, serial # 33376. 2. Henry rifle, 1860, serial #1705. 3. Winchester Saddle Ring carbine, 1866, serial #39711.

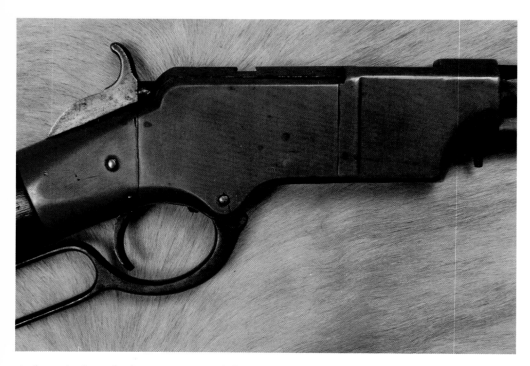

A closer look at the brass receiver of the Henry rifle.

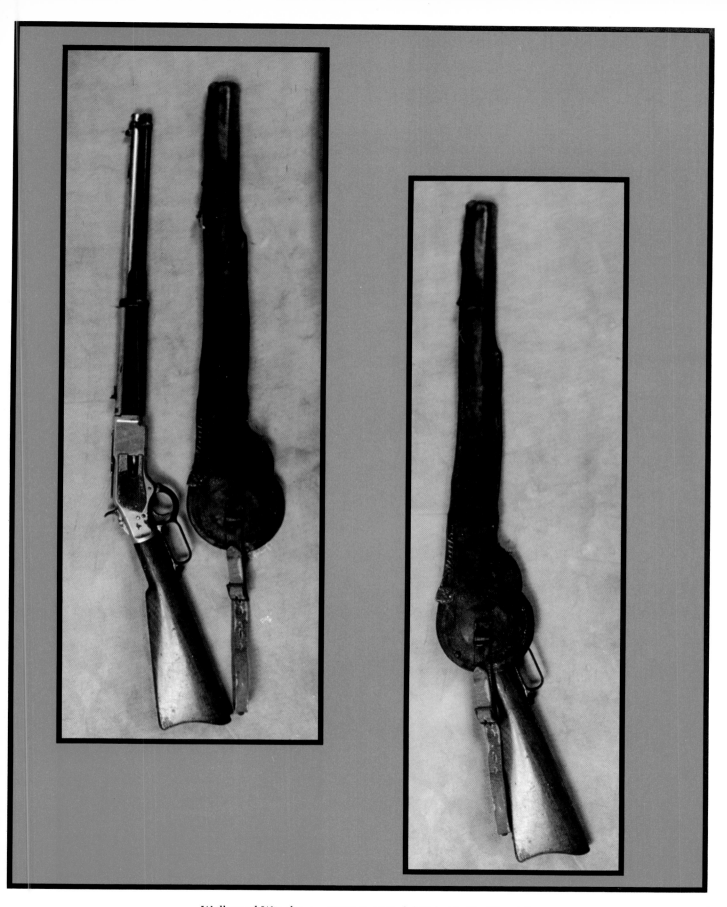

Well-used Winchester 1873 1st Model Cal .44-40 rifle with
the original scabbard. *Jonathan Peck.*

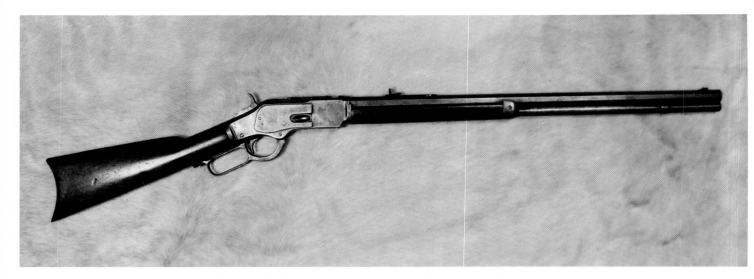

The justly famous Winchester model 1873 rifle with octagon barrel.

This Model 1873 Winchester Carbine was the cowboy's trusted companion in many tight situations. In caliber .44/40, the 20″ barrel made it a handy weapon. *Museum of Connecticut History.*

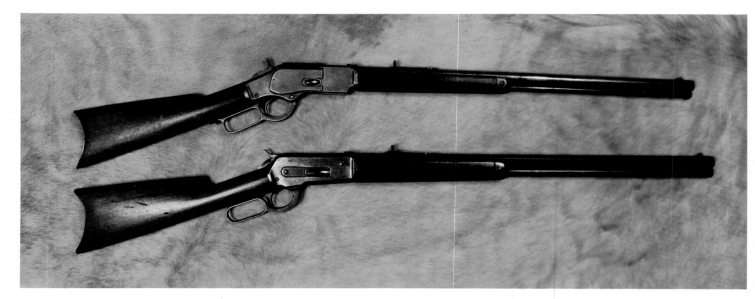

The top weapon is the Winchester 1873 with round barrel, while the bottom rifle is the Winchester 1886 rifle with octagon barrel.

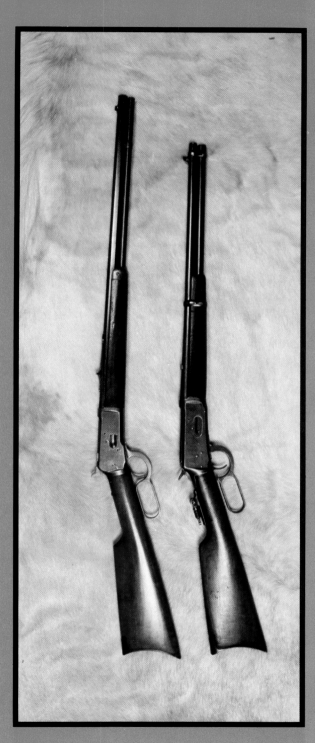

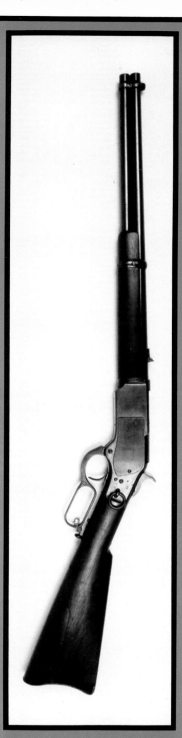

The Model 1886 Winchester Sporting rifle in caliber .45-90 was a favorite of the big game hunters of this period, including Teddy Roosevelt. *Museum of Connecticut History.*

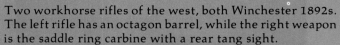

Two workhorse rifles of the west, both Winchester 1892s. The left rifle has an octagon barrel, while the right weapon is the saddle ring carbine with a rear tang sight.

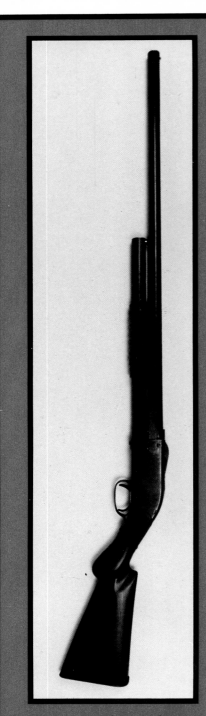

Developed around 1885, the 12 gauge Spencer Repeating shotgun with its 30" barrel, concealed hammer, and pump action was a great foraging weapon in the west. *Museum of Connecticut History.*

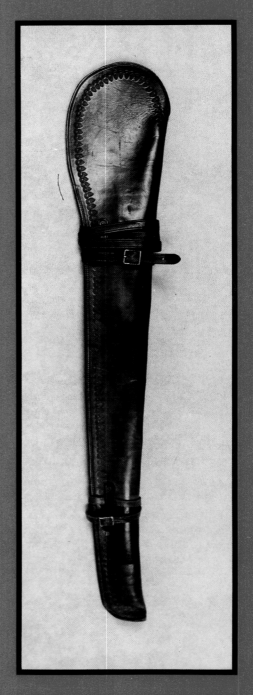

Decorated rifle scabbard, with tie-downs. While unmarked, it is probably for a Winchester.

Two tin gunpowder flasks. (Left) Mathewson's FFF gun powder, with (right) Indian Rifle powder made by E. I. DuPont de Nemours & Co.

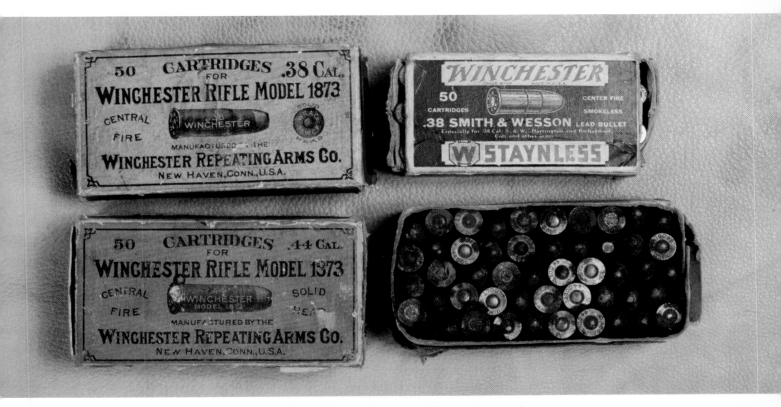

Boxed rifle and pistol cartridges; .44 caliber Colt cartridges are on the bottom row to the right.

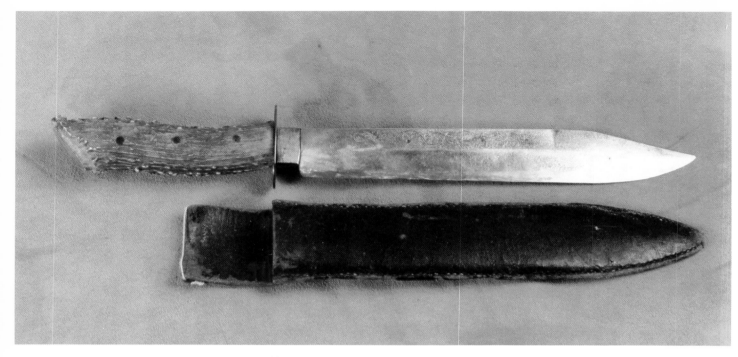

Massive gold miner's stag handled knife and sheath. The blade is engraved with the owner's initials, "T.L.S." on one side, while a pick and shovel are engraved on the reverse.

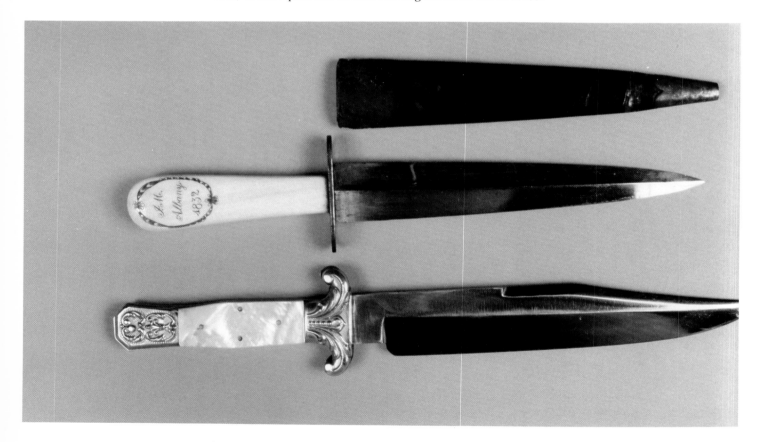

(Bottom) Bowie knife with pearl scales, silver mounted, by Luke Booth, mint condition. (Top) Straight blade Bowie knife with ivory scales, marked "Albany 1836." Excellent condition. *Larry Kaufman.*

Knives

In 1827, a man by the name of James Bowie became involved in personal and political differences between a Samuel Wells and a Doctor Thomas Maddox. On September 19, 1827, these differences erupted into the famous Vidalia Sandbar duel. In the parish of Concordia, across from Natchez, Louisiana, the participants and supporters met on a sandbar in the middle of the Mississippi river; after exchanging several shots, the duelists were satisfied, but their attending parties boiled over and a wild fight ensued. Bowie was shot down by Norris Wright, who rushed in to finish him off with a cane sword. Though grievously wounded, Bowie was able to pull out a large hunting knife and kill his opponent.

This launched the legend of the Bowie knife. The fight was reported in all its lurid details in the papers of the day, and men began asking for a knife "like Jim Bowie used." Immediately, blacksmiths and cutlers all over the South were besieged by requests to forge knives such as these, with the demand far outstripping the supply. The knife supplies of eastern cutlery dealers soon dwindled, and knifes were even made from old files. English cutlery firms, always on the lookout for new markets, rushed in to fill the void, with the result that many of the knives added to collections over the years were made by firms in Sheffield, England. American capacity for knife production was extremely limited and did not begin to come into its own, albeit on a very small scale, until the late 1830s, with the formation of the J. Russell & Co. -Green River Works in Massachusetts.

The popularity of the Bowie knife became so widespread that some southern states took steps to regulate their use. Tennessee, for example, passed severe laws with stringent penalties against the sale or use of "Bowie Knives and Arkansas Toothpicks in this state." During the war between the states, the long, Bowie-style knife was a favorite with Confederate troops, and many were made by local village blacksmiths.

On the frontier, the knife was an integral part of the cowboy's possessions. It received continuous hard use of a varied nature, ranging from fights and wars, to camp uses like cutting, chopping, digging, prying, cutting up game...and picking teeth. In later years large and unwieldy hunting knives were often ground down and shortened for easier use.

American firms producing knives included J. Russell & Co., Meriden Cutlery Co., Empire Knife Co., and Waterville Knife Co.

English firms were Thomas Elin, William Butcher, William Webster, F. T. Mappin, George Wostenholm, Henry Harrison, and Thomas Turner.

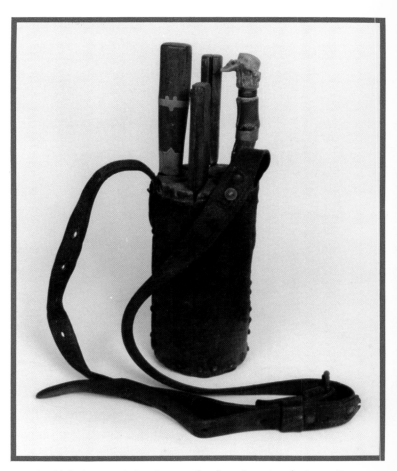

A buffalo hunter's knife case for his skinning knives. *Don Spaulding.*

A wonderful representation of frontier knives; from top to bottom:

1. Homemade skinning knife used by Lon Cale, buffalo hunter. 2. Homemade knife with brass guard and decorations. 3. Massive miner's Bowie knife with stag antler handle and etched decoration of miner's pick and shovel, with the initials T. L. S. 4. Butcher knife by J. Russell & Co., Green River Works. 5. Crude homemade butcher knife or machete.

Grouping of edged weapons used on the frontier. Top to bottom:

1. Stag horn small hunting knife 2. Skinning knife 3. Large Bowie knife as used by a Civil War officer, with lanyard ring. 4. Crude knife, possibly Indian made. Sent home by Lt. MacArthur during the 1870s from the Montana Territory. 5. Belt knife with pewter inlay. 6. Common style belt knife. 7. Stag horn, large bladed Bowie knife.

Some of the knives shown in the previous photos in their respective sheaths. Please note the differences from the crudely made to the well-decorated and finely fitted scabbards.

Branding Irons

As the crush of settlers moving westward grew, branding irons became a necessity for identifying individually owned herds of cattle. In the early days, this was accomplished with a straight piece wrought from a length of iron at an angle to the handle and used freehand to brand the animal. As time went on, stamp brands were developed that incorporated intricate designs. These artistic and handsomely detailed brands are much sought after...in fact, they are registered, taxed, and sold for high prices.

Made of iron with long handles finishing either in a closed loop for hanging, or with a wooden handle, brands vary greatly in intricacy as well as size. The larger irons are devoted to cattle and smaller ones are for use on horses. Among collectors, there is much greater interest in hand wrought irons as opposed to welded branding irons.

Buffalo skull with a group of branding irons. *Jonathan Peck.*

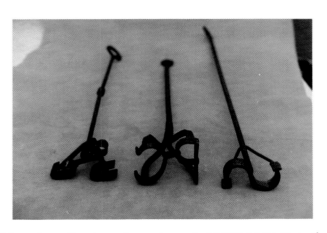

Three branding irons from the period 1875-1885. Note that the iron on the left is a very rare U.S. Cavalry iron.

Buffalo skull with another group of branding irons. *Jonathan Peck.*

Five very collectible branding irons, circa 1885. *Jonathan Peck/Ed Vebell.*

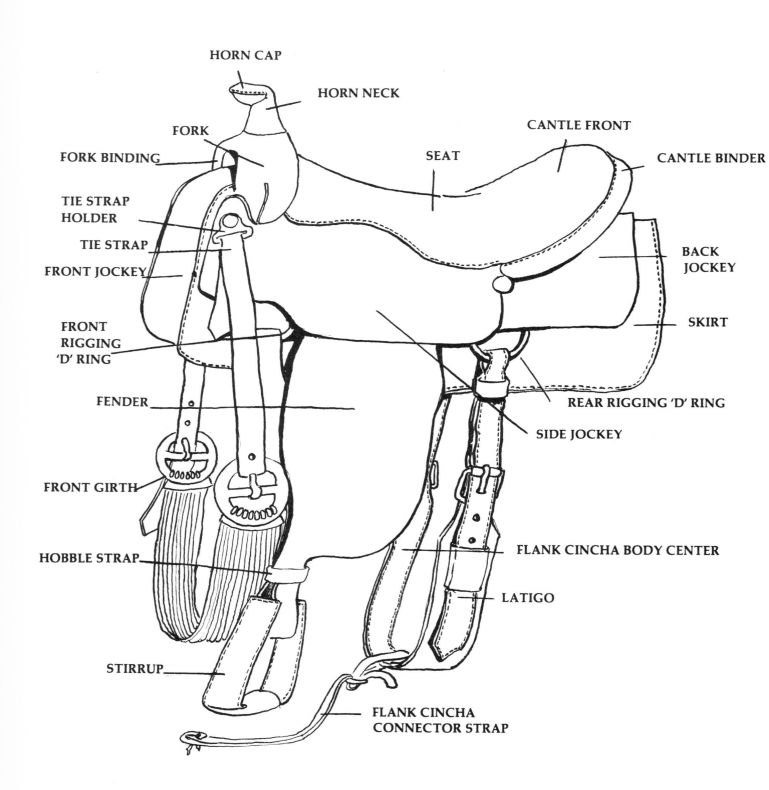

HORN CAP

HORN NECK

FORK

FORK BINDING

CANTLE FRONT

SEAT

CANTLE BINDER

TIE STRAP
HOLDER

TIE STRAP

FRONT JOCKEY

BACK
JOCKEY

FRONT
RIGGING
'D' RING

SKIRT

FENDER

REAR RIGGING 'D' RING

SIDE JOCKEY

FRONT GIRTH

FLANK CINCHA BODY CENTER

HOBBLE STRAP

LATIGO

STIRRUP

FLANK CINCHA
CONNECTOR STRAP

Saddles

including Bridles, Stirrups, Lariats and Saddle Bags

The working saddle of the West consists of a tree, or frame that forms the very basis of the saddle. Most often this was made of steel, covered in leather, on which is mounted the fork with horn, seat, and cantle, all leather bound. From the tree, skirts, tie straps, buckle straps, fenders, stirrup leathers, stirrups, and cinchas are made part of the saddle. Western saddles are especially adapted for ranch work, such as roping, bronco busting, and all forms of riding where the rider could be at risk. The swell fork and a high cantle provide the rider with a comfortable and safe seat at all times.

The heavy Mexican style saddle with a large horn and built like a rocking chair, was a favorite with cowboys. Evolving from the understandable need for comfort when spending seemingly endless daily hours on horseback, this saddle was a crucial link in the growth of the cattle industry.

In California, Indian saddles were the models for the saddle adopted by vaqueros, which eventually became the famous Visalia tree of the 1880s.

The 1870s saw the popularity of the *Mother Hubbard*. It was a large saddle with a low horn and a removable leather covering of the entire saddle (also referred to as a *Mochilo*).

In the 1880s the big *Plains* saddle, with it's square skirts, replaced the *Mother Hubbard*. Separate seat jockeys became popular around 1885.

During the latter part of the century, styles such as the Plains saddle, the Vaquero and others began to meld, until saddle makers were customizing saddles to a customer's wishes with a blend of styles for every taste. This is understandable. Since the saddle was as necessary to the cowboy as his horse, the choice of saddle became a very personal matter, akin to having clothing tailor-made. At the end of the day, it became his back rest around the campfire; at night, it became his pillow. Along with his pistol and rifle, the saddle was one of the biggest purchases made in the life of a cowpoke.

To put it simply, a bridle is a leather harness that goes over the head of the horse. This holds the bit, which is attached to the reins for controlling the horse. Once again, the harness could be decorated and made as fancy as the cowboy's pocket would allow. Several fancy outfits are illustrated.

"The Rescue," by Don Spaulding. Don Spaulding combines his love of the cavalry with his predilection for human interest subjects. This is due to his training while a student of Norman Rockwell.

A western half-seat saddle variation of the "Hope" design of around 1855, showing its Southwest and Mexican influence. *Don Spaulding.*

Hope saddle from the 1850s; generally referred to as the Spanish saddle. Used by many army officers during the Civil War. This saddle was one of the forerunners of the cowboy saddle. *Don Spaulding.*

1850s era rawhide covered saddle, double rigged, Sam Stagg rigging. *Don Spaulding.*

1880s double rigged half seat saddle, with Sam Stagg rigging. Note the basket stamping over the entire saddle. *Don Spaulding.*

1870s "Mother Hubbard" style saddle, typical of the "Trail Drive" era saddles. Skirt is marked "V.E. Vaughn. Austin Tex." *Don Spaulding.*

Close-up of makers stamping on "Mother Hubbard" saddle. *Don Spaulding.*

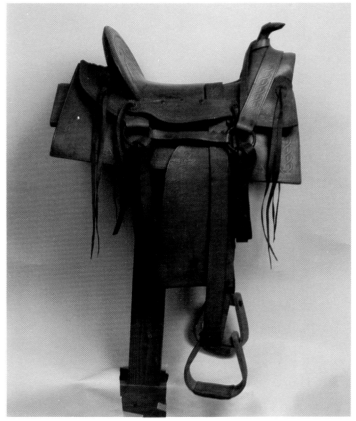

High backed saddle from the 1880s. Double rigged, half seat, Sam Stagg rigging. Reportedly used by a sheriff in Montana. *Don Spaulding.*

A well-preserved Coggshall saddle, made by Miles City Saddlery Co., Miles City, Montana. Note the swell fork, the single rig, and the conchos.

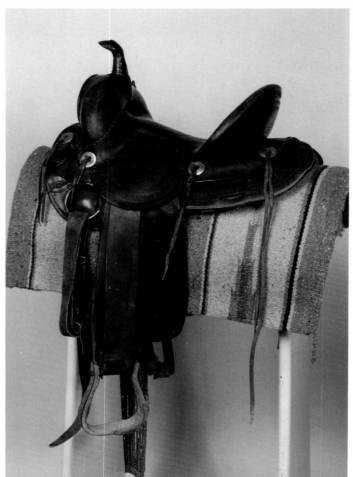

Idaho Territory Saddle, circa 1880s. Retains the original monkey-nose Tapaderos. This saddle was probably made by the Logan Brothers of Grangeville, Idaho Territory, and was used on the John Day Ranch. Authenticated by Bob Byrd of the High Desert Museum, Bend, Oregon. *Jerard Paul Jordan Galleries/M.L. Gardner Photography.*

Model 1885 cavalry saddle completely outfitted for campaign with saddle bags, carbine boot, and saddle blanket, with the blanket roll inside of nose bag. *Don Spaulding.*

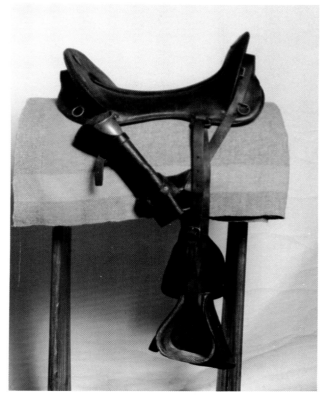

A lovely lightweight single rig, high backed "A" frame saddle. Note the stamping on all the leathers. No maker's name.

A nicely ornamented high cantle saddle with high brass horn made by the R.T. Frazier Co. of Pueblo, Colorado. Circa 1895-1900.

An especially nice model 1885 McClellan black leather cavalry saddle, with the 1885 carbine boot. The brass throat of the boot is to cut down on wear from the carbine hammer.

Stirrups are attached to the saddle fenders and are for placement of the feet when in the saddle. They are made from all sorts of material, ranging from steamed and bent wood to iron and steel. They can be leather covered in the style of the Mexican tapaderos which protect the foot and lower leg from thorns and brush, or they may be simply purely utilitarian in design.

Lariats had countless uses in the West. The better ones were handmade from leather strips carefully woven together to produce a rope with great tensile strength, yet with give. Many of these have lasted well over one hundred years in excellent condition. These lariats were used for lassoing cattle as well as horses, and were always to be found with the cowboy's saddle.

An integral part of the cowboy's equipment were his saddle bags, carrying the meager essentials that the cowboy needed while on the range. Most often made of leather, they consisted of two separate bags connected by a yoke that went across the neck of the horse. This allowed a bag to rest on either side of the horse's neck, thereby balancing the load.

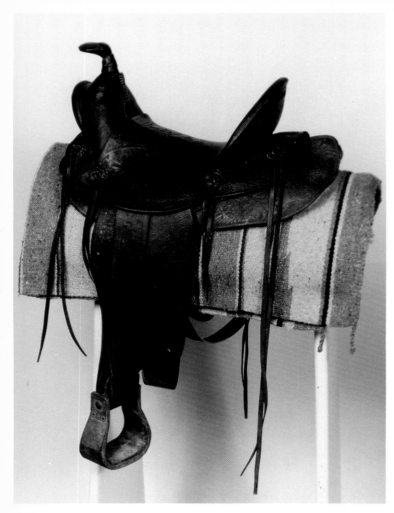

Floral tooled, single rig, high backed "A" frame saddle, made by Wade & Co., San Francisco, California.

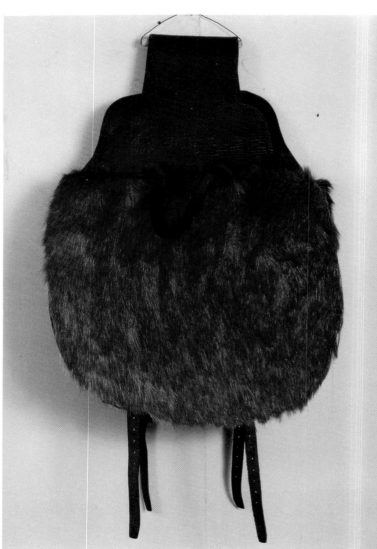

Hide-out saddle bags, circa 1900. *Jerard Paul Jordan Galleries/M.L. Gardner Photography.*

A prime example of an unmarked common working cowboy's single rig, high cantle saddle. This saddle dates from the turn of the century.

A beautifully executed high cantle saddle by Frank Meanea.
Jerard Paul Jordon Galleries/M.L. Gardner Photography.

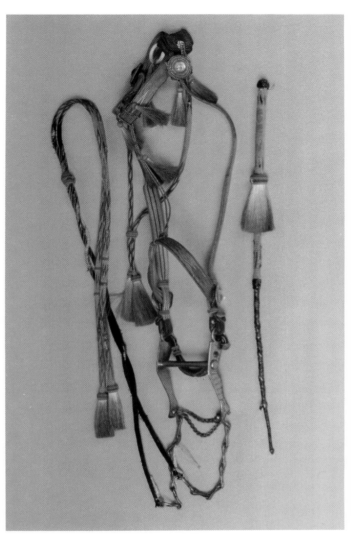

Braided horsehair bridle and quirt, with a "Gal-Leg" bit.
Jonathan Peck.

Painting of "Apaches Stealing Horses" by Carl Hantman. A full-size preliminary sketch done prior to the final painting, this sketch shows Carl Hantman's mastery of color and atmosphere.

Miniature saddle used as a salesman's sample. Unusual and rare. *Jonathan Peck.*

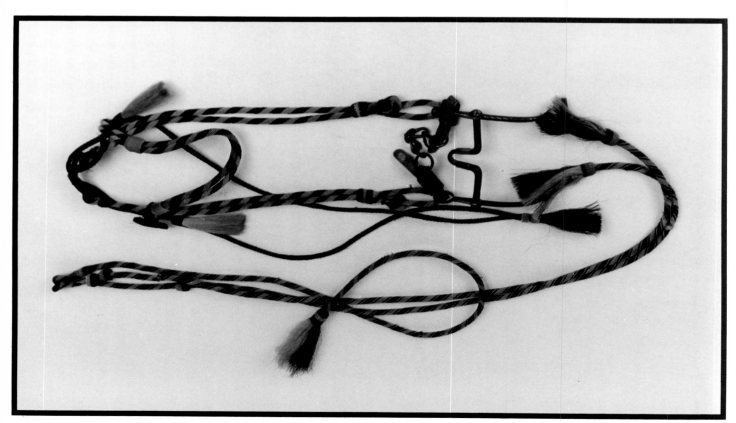

Braided horsehair bridle made in southwestern prison prior to the turn of the century.

Bridle with studded cheek straps and painted horse heads as bosses. *Don Spaulding.*

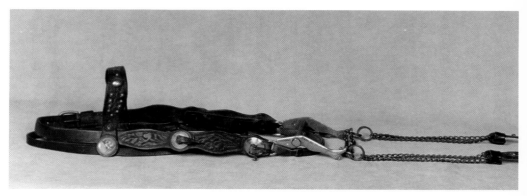

Concho decorated tooled bridle with "Gal-Leg" bit. *Don Spaulding.*

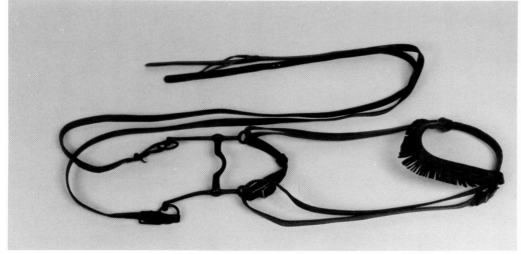

Old, simple lightweight bridle.

Unusual bridle of rolled and stitched leather, instead of the usual flat leathers. Stamped "E.T. Frazier, Pueblo, Colo."

Brass bit with silver heart decorations, as well as brass and silver nose decorations. *Jonathan Peck.*

Matching martingale with brass and silver decorations. *Jonathan Peck.*

Bridle with floral stamped design.

Bridle of German silver conchos and studs. Stamped "Miles City Saddlery-Miles City, Mont."

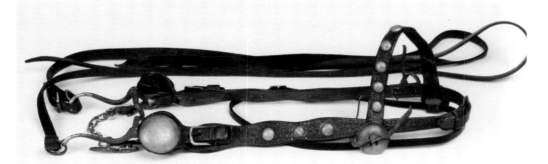

A highly prized, prison made, braided bridle with silver decorations on the bit, consisting of Spades, Hearts, Diamonds and Clubs. *Jonathan Peck.*

A great pair of highly tooled, "Monkey Nose" Tapaderos stirrups, with thong-tied concho. *Don Spaulding.*

California-style Tapaderas. *Jonathan Peck.*

A braided lariat.

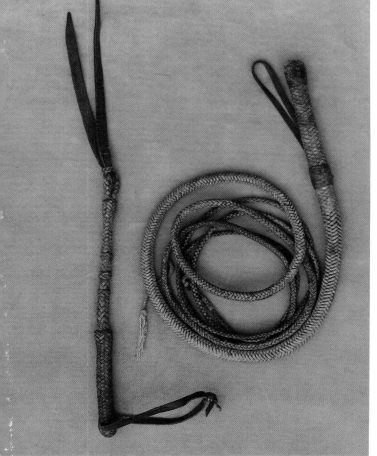

A bull whip or possibly a coach whip, in excellent condition, along with a great braided quirt.

A braided lariat in excellent condition.

A fine pair of saddle bags, circa 1890, heavily decorated with nickel studs.

Saddle bags signed "Kings Ranch," circa 1900. A beautiful pair of saddle bags marked "Kings Ranch—Running W brand—Kingsville, Texas" on each pocket flap. With the exception of a missing pocket strap, these bags are in excellent condition. *Jerard Paul Jordan Galleries/M.L. Gardner Photography.*

Physician's saddle bag. This saddle bag is a patent model, one of 14, with patent tags from the years 1869, 1870, and 1881. By G. W. Elliott. *Jerard Paul Jordan Galleries/M.L. Gardner Photography.*

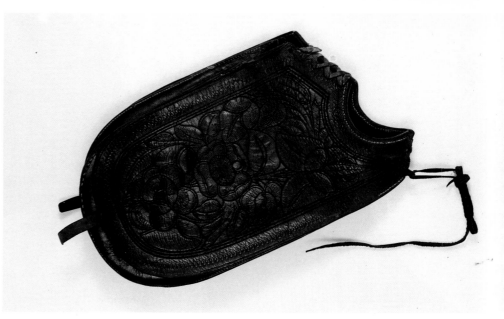

Saddle bags, signed "Johnson." *Jerard Paul Jordan Galleries/M.L. Gardner Photography.*

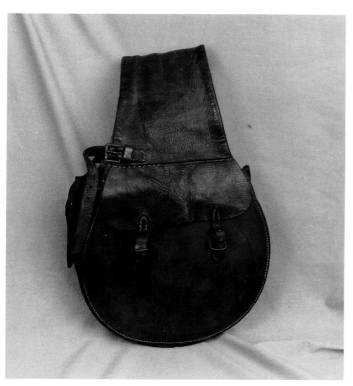

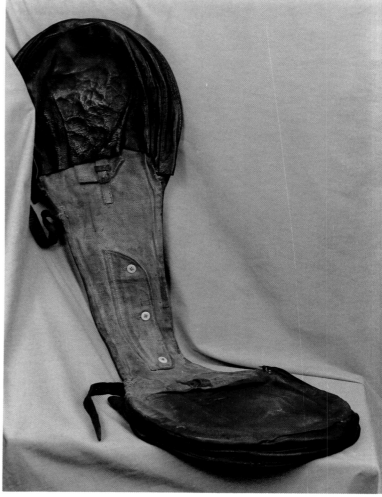

Representative saddle bags. *Jerard Paul Jordan Galleries/M.L. Gardner Photography.*

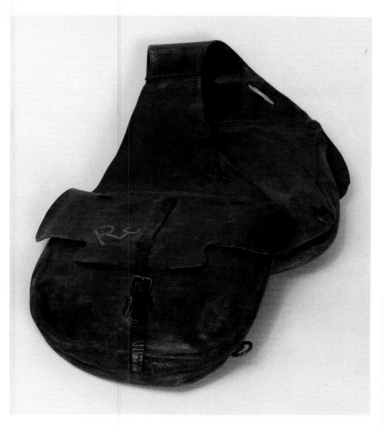

Civilian saddle bags made by removing the two retaining straps from each bag of a United Sates Model 1904 set of cavalry saddle bags.

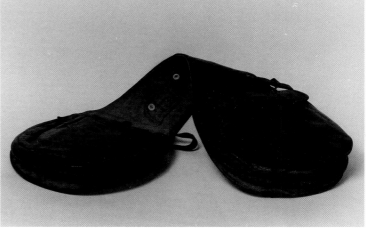

Civilian saddle bags with a canvas liner and a flapped interior pouch on the underside.

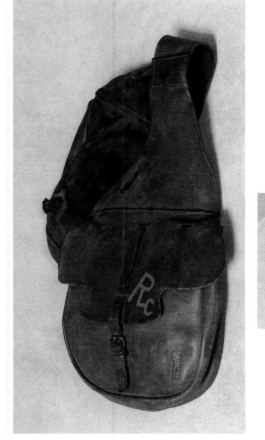

Note the concealed buttoned down pocket for valuables.

(Right) Double full-bodied "Gal-Leg" spurs, with Star of Texas rowels. (Left) "Gal-Leg" bit by August Buermann. *Jonathan Peck.*

Salesman's sample of "Gal Leg".

(Right) Silver mounted Spade bit, marked "Pendleton." (Left) California Spade bit by Buermann. *Jonathan Peck.*

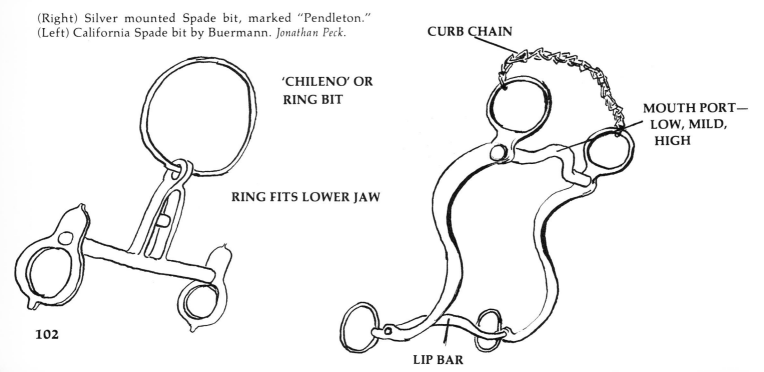

'CHILENO' OR RING BIT

RING FITS LOWER JAW

CURB CHAIN

MOUTH PORT— LOW, MILD, HIGH

LIP BAR

Bits

The use of a bit for controlling horses goes back to antiquity. As a piece of Western Americana, these metal parts of the bridle are highly collectible and those that are signed and/or marked by their makers command impressive prices.

By looking at the bit in a horse's mouth, it was not difficult to determine a cowboy's origins. To the west of the Rockies cowboys used the heavy Spanish spade bit, brought north by the Vaqueros out of Mexico. These spade bits evolved into several other styles. The "half-breed" bit has a roller or cricket in the mouth port. It is also possible to find the ring bit, or "Chileno," consisting of an iron ring that fits the mouth port and circles under the chin, thereby acting as a curb strap. The ornate California spade bit is a highly desirable collectible. This is not usually maker-marked, but is hand-made, blued, and often has a silver inlay. If the bit does happen to be marked, it will undoubtedly bring a premium. Later bits were usually machine made, showing less aesthetic care in the production and were most often maker-marked.

To the east of the Rockies, the plains cowboy favored the curb bit. The U. S. Model 1859 and the later Shoemaker bits were the most popular for breaking a horse. The plains bit has solid or moveable rings for attaching leather reins, while the Texas curb bit has a short, curved shank bit with solid rings. One of the favorite styles over many years has been the "Gal-Leg" bit, which has side pieces in the form of a woman's leg. The side pieces lent themselves to a personalized art form. The buyer was limited only by the money he wanted to spend and the skill of the craftsman.

Bits were made in innumerable styles and finishes. They are found blued, japanned, plain burnished, plain nickel, burnished and chased, nickel and chased, plated, and polished. Bits have been made with a spade mouth or a port mouth. The ports could have been low ports, mild ports or high ports, with or without rollers (also known as *crickets*), as well as with rein chains if desired.

Since 1842, one of the most outstanding manufacturers of bits and spurs has been the August Buermann Mfg. Co. of Newark, New Jersey, justly famous for their *Star* brand. This company was purchased after World War One by North & Judd Manufacturing Co. of New Britain, Connecticut another old-time firm devoted to the manufacture of harness, baggage, belt, and blanket hardware, and famous for their fine wrought products.

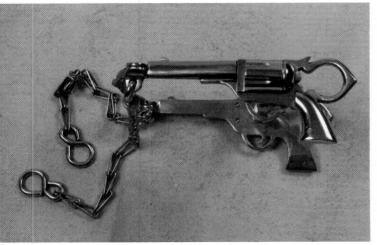

Buffalo Bill bit with full-bodied Colt Single Action revolvers. *Jonathan Peck.*

Mexican silvered spade bit. *Steve Crowley..*

Well-used, but still serviceable Mexican spurs with large, blunt rowels. *Don Spaulding*.

Southwestern style spurs with what appear to be Mexican style rowels and jingles. *Don Spaulding*.

Brass and steel spurs marked "Don Ricardo." Mexican-style leather straps.

Spurs

Simply put, spurs are worn on the back of a rider's boots and are used to make a horse go forward. The spur consists of a *heel band* that slides onto the counter of the boot and is held in place by the *spur strap*. Spurs with straight heel bands are called *straight-button spurs*; spurs with upward curving bands are called *raised-button spurs*. The *spur strap* and *heel chains* are attached to the *spur button*, which can be either fixed or swinging.

Basically, there are three different types of shanks: *straight shanks, raised shanks, and dropped shanks*. Most ordinary riders prefer drop-shank spurs, while bronco-busters and tall riders are more apt to favor raised-shank spurs for the very practical reason that they make more rapid contact with the horse. As a point of vanity, some shanks, made in the shape of a woman's leg, were called *Gal-leg*, while others featured *gooseneck, horse-head* or *eagle* patterns.

A rounded *chap hook*, intended to keep a rider's chaps from becoming entangled in the spur rowels, is frequently found on the upper part of the shank. *Rowels*, which were pinned in a slot at the far end of the shank, came in a variety of spoke wheels containing anywhere from five to twenty points, and were also crafted in a saw tooth pattern.

Early California, vaquero, or buckaroo spurs retain the influences of the conquistadors, having straight solid-button heel bands and retaining the drop shank. From Mexico came the heavy spurs known as *Chihuahuas*, with wide heel bands, swing buttons and spoke rowels. Texas spur makers of the same era were also making their mark in western history. Influenced somewhat by the Chihuahua style, Texas spurs can be found with wide oval bands, swing buttons (which do not press into the rider's ankle), spoke rowels, straight unornamented shanks, and chap hooks or guards. Spurs with long shanks without chap hooks have often been regarded as *Rocky Mountain* spurs.

Among collectors, prison-made spurs are highly prized for the intricate, time-consuming inlay work that usually sets them apart from their less flashy counterparts. As a means of earning some money while incarcerated, prisoners in western prisons during the latter part of the 1800s were allowed to make fancy bits, spurs, and bridles for sale.

All of these influences have merged and melded over the last century, resulting in beautiful collector pieces incorporating the best features of many different styles of spur making.

(Right) Chihuahua spurs, Mexican shanks inlaid with pesos; rowels are southwestern style. These were found in Tombstone, Arizona. (Left) Nevada style spurs, silver inlay with large silver buttons. *Jonathan Peck.*

Engraved spurs marked "STAR STEEL SILVER." Note the stamped designs on the leather straps.

Nevada-style spurs with silver buttons and small rowels from Missoula, Montana. *Jonathan Peck.*

Spurs by Kelly Brothers, Texas. Arrows pointing up, original leathers. *Jonathan Peck.*

Well-used spurs with conchos. Unsigned. *Don Spaulding.*

Colorado prison made spurs, finely engraved with silver buttons. These spurs were used on the Johnson Ranch, Olathe, Colorado. *Jonathan Peck.*

Pair of brass spurs with silver Buffalo Heads. *Jonathan Peck.*

Steel spurs with leather straps marked "H.B. brand,
HARPHAM BROS. Co., LINCOLN, NEBRASKA."

Simply engraved spurs with danglers.

Spurs with large, hand-forged rowels. The leather straps
have been replaced over the years.

Engraved steel spurs, marked
"Pat'd. * "

Engraved spurs with danglers and simple working straps.
Spurs are marked with patent date of 1877.

(Left) Spurs with heart designs made by Crockett. Spur
straps stamped "War Nock-New York, established 1888."
(Right) Ornate spurs with large conchas made by Crockett.

U.S. Cavalry scene by Don Spaulding. Spaulding's extensive knowledge of the U.S. Cavalry and the Indian War period brings forth extremely accurate and brilliantly painted scenes of the Old West. Oil on gesso panel.

A fine collection of the effects of a doctor in service with the 1st Cavalry. Note the inclusion of the color green (signifying medical service) with the cavalry yellow.

The United States Army

Policemen of the Plains
(1865—1890)

During the Civil War, the West was simmering with a series of Indian Wars that made what came before look like mere rehearsals. Approximately 20,000 volunteers were recruited in the territories for home defense. While subduing some tribes in their hard-hitting manner, these citizen soldiers also stirred up many others. The Regulars who relieved them at the end of the Civil War inherited a hate-filled powder keg.

Every raid and depredation by Indians raised a stormy chorus for military retaliation. With the continuing flow of emigrants during the Civil War, the West was beginning to turn into a powerful lobby. On July 28, 1866, President Johnson became the first chief executive to expand the U. S. Army immediately following a war. Artillery remained at its wartime levels, while the infantry went from 19 to 45 regiments, of which four regiments were Negro enlisted men. The cavalry went from 6 regiments to 10, of which 2 were Negro enlisted men with white officers. The Army Appropriation Act of 1869 then reduced the infantry by 20 regiments and shrunk the cavalry companies to 60 privates each. In 1874 the annual appropriations act limited the standing army to 27,000, including officers. The only event that temporarily contravened this limitation was the almost complete annihilation of the 7th Cavalry at the battle of the Little Big Horn on June 25, 1876.

The "Queen of Battle," the infantry, was always the poor relation on the frontier. Throughout the Indian wars, the long-suffering infantry shouldered more than its share of the fighting. In 1869, there were about 200 posts to be manned, which spread the fighting forces rather thin. In any event, when hostilities flared, the local post involved had to be heavily reinforced before any punitive expeditions could be dispatched.

Frustration was rampant. The officers were heavily overburdened with responsibilities due to commands being consistently understaffed with officers, while all ranks suffered the nature of the warfare: coming to grips with the enemy. The Indian was supremely equipped as a hit-and-run guerilla fighter, while the army on the frontier was a conventional army requiring a wide logistical base. It took George Crook, a student of Indian thinking and tactics to make the changes and innovations necessary to fight the Indian on a more

Model 1872 officer's un-dress uniform coat belonging to a staff officer with the rank of major. Also shown are a pair of hide cavalry gauntlets. *Don Spaulding.*

U.S. cavalry dress uniform of 1873 for the 2nd Cavalry, including the dress helmet with retaining cords and the original uncut visor at the rear of the helmet.

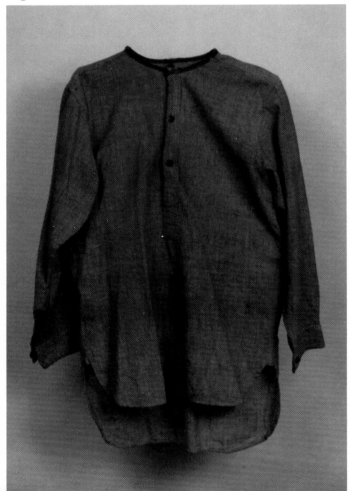

equal footing. By perseverance and cunning, he helped change the rules of warfare and brought the fight home to the Indian.

Ten hard years of this kind of fighting began to take its toll on the Plains Indian; their entire existence became fighting and fleeing, with fewer and fewer places to hide. Some bands surrendered, while others chose to stand and fight to the death.

Life in the army during the Indian Wars was never easy. There were too few men for the tasks involved, and the overall quality of the troopers was poor, with very little time spent on basic training. To compound the problem, marksmanship was terrible due to the government's penurious policies of allowing only a trickle of funds for things as basic as target practice. Little wonder that desertion rates were sky high, while re-enlistments of trained men were meager.

There was one bright spot, however. As Gregory J.W. Urwin so graphically expressed in "The United States Cavalry; An illustrated History":

> "Nowhere were the qualities of instant courage, good humor under adversity, devotion to duty and lasting loyalty displayed to better advantage in the Indian-Fighting Army than among the two black mounted regiments, the 9th and 10th Cavalry. On account of the prevailing white prejudice of the day, their exploits were ignored or belittled, and they were subjected to indignities that made the lowly lot of their pale-faced colleagues look luxurious. Harried by Army and Civilian authorities, they were given old and damaged equipment, broken-down nags that had been lamed by other outfits or purchased during the Civil War, the most miserable quarters and the dirtiest jobs on the frontier. Derided by their white comrades as 'Moacs,' 'Brunettes' and 'Niggers,' they were called 'Buffalo Soldiers' by the Indians for their tight curly hair and fierce fighting spirit."[2]

During the Indian Wars, individuality expressed itself in many non-regulation ways, especially in the manner of dress that was adopted by the troops, not only in the various units, but also individually, with many uniforms being personally designed by the wearer. A favorite among officers and men alike for campaign use was the flannel "firemen's shirt," while privately purchased hats, cravats, sun helmets, Apache-style leggings and hardy buckskin coats were often to be found. This is not to say that there was no uniformity of dress, but simply to illustrate the fact that men adapted to the conditions on the frontier.

Cavalry shirt used in the 1870s. It was the common practice of soldiers to cut off the collar; this then became standard issue in 1879. *Don Spaulding.*

Sergeant's five-button infantry sack coat, circa 1875-1880. The lining is reminiscent of the Civil War cloth, and the coat came with a pair of trousers, as shown.

Officer's un-dress coat of 1895 for the 3rd Cavalry, as well as matching trousers. The ribbon bars read, from the top and left to right: Army Distinguished Service Medal, Society of Cincinnati, Mexican Border Service, WWI Victory Medal with 2 stars, Panamanian "La Solidaridad," France-Chevalier, Legion d'Honneur, France-Croix de Guerre with star, France-WWI Commemorative, Poland-The Cross of Merit.

Model 1895 infantry officer's un-dress coat with trousers; insignia for the 11th Infantry. The inside of the pocket has the name of the owner, Major Quimby, Fort Apache, 1897.

(Left) Campaign hat, Model 1872, for officers and enlisted men. This could be worn with the brim down as shown, or hooked up on the sides. This hat was short-lived as it was thoroughly disliked by one and all. It was considered to be a complete failure due to disintegration. (Right) Officer's kepi with embroidered bullion crossed sabers. Circa 1865-1872.

Cavalry enlisted man's kepi, "F" Troop, circa 1870-1880. *Don Spaulding.*

Model 1883 cavalry shirt of dark blue wool flannel. *Don Spaulding.*

Cavalry officer's Model 1872 dress helmet, as well as three personal items belonging to Captain F.W. Benteen, 7th Cavalry. *Don Spaulding*.

Model 1872 cavalry officer's dress helmet, which is lacking the regimental number. *Don Spaulding*.

Model 1890 Indian Scouts' dress helmet, with distinctive colored cords. *Don Spaulding*.

115

Cavalry officer's model slouch hat, circa 1885, with unusual star badge attached to the side of the crown. *Don Spaulding.*

Model 1881 dress cavalry helmet (enlisted) for the 5th Cavalry, with yellow retaining cords. *Don Spaulding.*

Campaign slouch hat for enlisted men, circa 1885. Note ventilators on the sides of the hat. *Don Spaulding.*

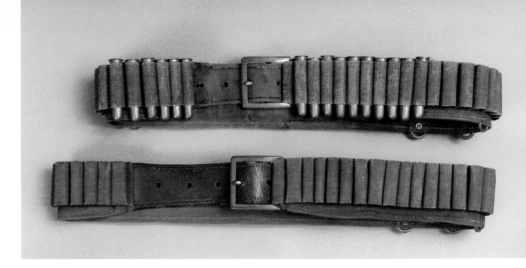

Two different styles of "Prairie" belts for the 45-70 cartridge, circa 1870-1880.

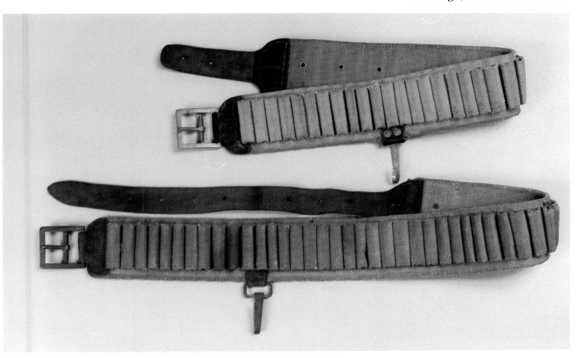

Top: Model 1881 Cavalry Mills Woven Cartridge belt, 40 loops, .45/70. *Robert Dailey.* Bottom: Model 1881 Cavalry Mills Woven Cartridge belt, 45 loops, .45/70. *Robert Dailey.*

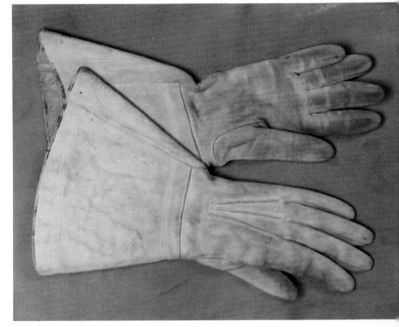

A pair of post-Civil War period cavalry officer's cuffed gauntlets.

(Left) RIA Carbine Rig, circa 1867. *Robert Dailey.* (Right) Field Artillery Model 1873 Carbine scabbard, mint condition. *Larry Kaufman.*

Model 1885 cavalry saddle blanket with 1885 bridle and Shoemaker bit. *Don Spaulding.*

Enlisted man's belt, buckle, and cap pouch in mint condition. *Larry Kaufman.*

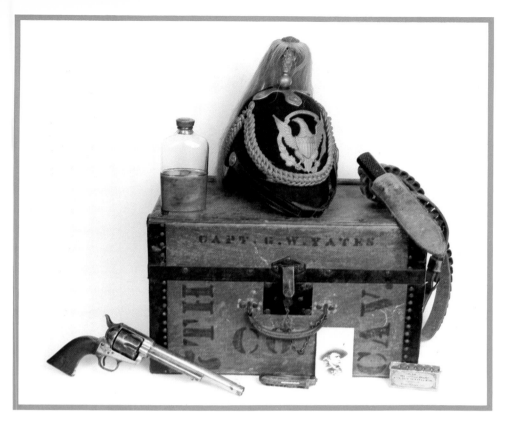

Cavalry artifacts, including a Model 1872 cavalry officer's dress helmet, Captain Benteen's pistol, flask, box of pistol cartridges, field belt with knife and sheath, carte-de-visite of General George A. Custer, all grouped around the field chest of Captain George Yates of the 7th cavalry. *Don Spaulding.*

The field chest of Captain George Yates, commander of Company "F," 7th Cavalry. Captain Yates was killed with General Custer at the battle of the Little Big Horn. *Don Spaulding.*

Interior view of the field chest of Captain Yates, showing the Horstmann & Co. label. *Don Spaulding.*

HERE FELL CUSTER

"Here Fell Custer," by Eric Von Schmidt. An epic work of research and reconstruction, measuring 5 feet high by 13 feet in length. This is considered the definitive depiction of the Custer massacre. Acrylic on linen canvas. *Ulrich Museum of Art, Wichita, Kansas.*

Carte-de-Visite photo of General George A. Custer. 2¼" x 3½" without markings of any sort.

Cabinet photo of General George A. Custer. 4" x 6".

Matthew Brady photos of General George A. Custer. 2¾" x
3¾". Mounts are marked "162" and "164."

The revolver, flask, and pocket knife belonging to Captain
F.W. Benteen of Little Big Horn fame. *Don Spaulding*.

Cabinet photo of Lt. James Calhoun, L Troop, 7th Cavalry. A hardworking officer who worked himself up through the ranks to a commission.

Cabinet photo of Lt. Tom Custer, brother of Lt. Col. George A. Custer, 7th Cavalry, shown wearing his two Medals of Honor. As a captain, he was killed along with his brother at the Battle of the Little Big Horn, 25 June 1876.

Cabinet signed photo of cavalrymen of the 1880-1890 period.

Express Company Memorabilia

The delivery of packages and parcels by express companies started in the East during the late 1830s, and with the discovery of gold in 1848 the business rapidly spread to the Pacific coast. The action in California was dominated for a number of years by the Adams Express Company. Henry Wells and William G. Fargo felt that there was room for competition, and in 1852 Wells Fargo & Co., a banking and express company, was chartered in San Francisco.

After the bank panic of 1855, the Adams Express Company was crippled and forced to close its doors in California, while Wells Fargo was in a solvent position, enabling it to become the leading banking and express company in the state. In 1857, Wells Fargo became involved with the Overland Mail Co., acting as it's banker. Overburdened with debt in 1860, Overland Mail Co. was taken over by Wells Fargo, which continued to prosper despite the unstable financial climate of the previous decade.

In 1861, a government contract was awarded to the newly-acquired Overland Mail Company for a Pony Express on the central route; Wells Fargo meanwhile was operating the western leg of the Pony Express. The Pony Express was forced out of business with the completion of the transcontinental telegraph in October of 1861, even though Wells Fargo continued the Western division from Virginia City, Nevada to Sacramento, California until 1865. Only in existence for 18 months, the Pony Express nevertheless left an indelible mark on this period of American history, and its name has become almost generic when referring to the transport of the mails through the Old West.

Ever alert to the winds of change, Wells Fargo realized that with the completion of the transcontinental railway, their days as a stage coach company were numbered. In October of 1869, a contract between the railroad and Wells Fargo was hammered out that guaranteed a new era of prosperity for Wells Fargo, creating one of the largest banking and express companies in America. In 1906, the banking operation was split from that of the express company, and Wells Fargo became one of the leading banks in California.

In order to help bring World War I to a speedy conclusion, the four major express companies—American, Adams, Southern, and Wells Fargo—were merged by Presidential order into the American Railway Express Co. In 1929, this name was changed to the Railway Express Agency; in 1960, it became R. E. A. Express, continuing for only fifteen more years before going into bankruptcy in 1975.

Artifacts of the express companies, such as signs, logos, dispatch bags, firearms, badges, seals, and stamps, as well as innumerable paper items, still can be found at reasonable prices. As in many other fields of collecting, reproductions are making an unwelcome appearance, so the collector must be ever alert for fakes.

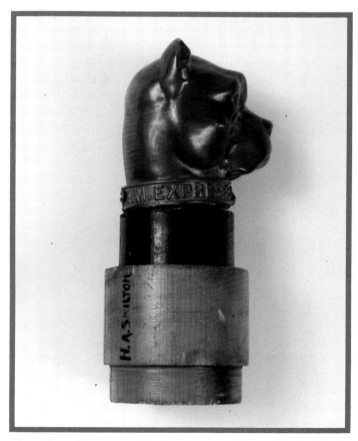

American Express collection cup and logo Dog's Head. *Jonathan Peck.*

"The Pony Express." This was done by Ed Vebell as one of 150 paintings for the Postal Commemorative Society of Norwalk, Connecticut. It was recreated by models in full costume on horseback. Oil on gesso panel.

An original Wells Fargo Express leather mail bag, in excellent condition.

Collection of American Express memorabilia. *Jonathan Peck.*

An illustration by Ed Vebell for the Postal Commemorative
Society, "First Overland Mail."

A rarity in this condition! A serially numbered Wells Fargo horse blanket. The lettering appears on both sides of the blanket.

Waybill of the U.S. Mail Line in 1867 between Marysville, California and Sacramento, California.

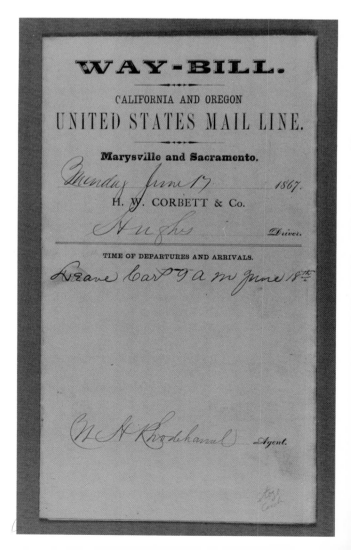

Original American express sign. *Jonathan Peck.*

American Express grouping, including pistol with "American Express" on the back strap. *Jonathan Peck.*

A close look at a rare American Express driver's badge. *Jonathan Peck.*

Close-up of American Express pistol showing the engraving on the backstrap. *Jonathan Peck.*

Two color western illustration by Ed Vebell. Used for Time-
Life series books as a promotional mailer.

Common and Uncommon Items Found in the West

We have tried to show a multitude of items from everyday life on the frontier as it was known to our ancestors, whether it be tools from the ranch, poker chips found in the saloon, or the miner's sluice pan. As mundane as some these things may be, they all go to make up our Western heritage.

Some of the most poignant images of the past are caught in the staged formality of the cabinet photos still available to us today...the seriousness of youth rigged out with rifle and pistol, our knowledge of the fate that awaited certain army officers as they sat for their pictures before the battle of the Little Big Horn, and the realization that the generations apart have so much in common with one another.

...and so continues our everlasting romance with the spirit of the West.

1908-1910 Nevada State Prison "mug shots" and descriptions of prisoners. Handcuffs are marked "Hiatt Best—warranted wrought." To the right is an original "Special Officer" badge.

Brass leg irons, marked "Judd." Below, is a rare Colt U. S. Single Action revolver barracks brass hanger. *Larry Kaufman.*

Representative sheriff and marshal's badges from the frontier period.

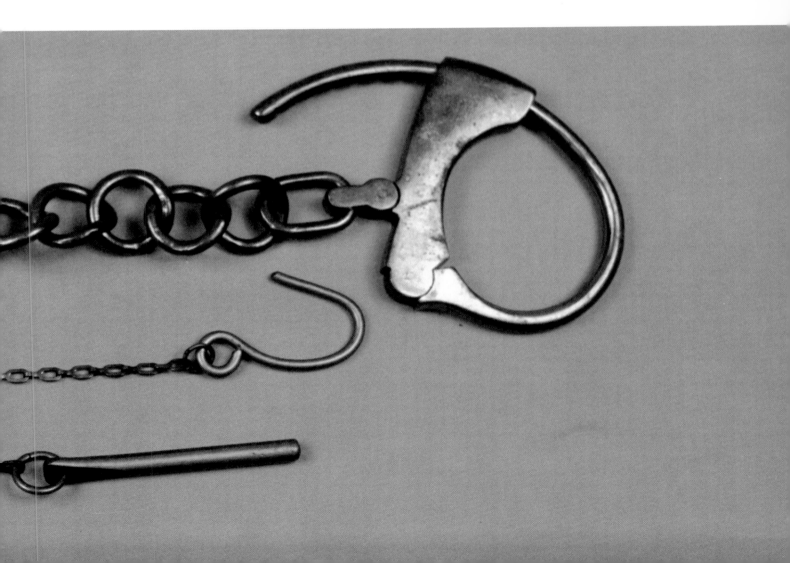

Grouping of original representative badges. *Jonathan Peck.*

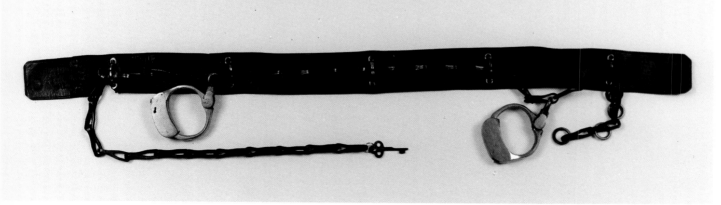

Restraining belt with handcuffs and lead along chain; marked "F.A. Hyatt, Alamosa, Colorado. 1886." *Jonathan Peck.*

Two pairs of handcuffs and a set of leg irons. The leg irons are marked "Towers Double Lock." *Steve Crowley.*

This Cyrus Noble Whiskey advertisement illustrates a scene at the Old Orient Saloon in Bishee, Arizona in 1890. *Steve Crowley.*

A great trio of whiskey bottles, circa 1880. *Steve Crowley.*

Faro Table, circa 1890. The dealer sits in the slot in the foreground, while the "counter" works the abacus-like from on the opposite side. *Steve Crowley.*

Barroom whiskey decanters with their brand names lettered on the glass. *Don Spaulding.*

Gambling items, including an innocent looking book hollowed out to contain a pocket derringer, handmade ivory poker chips, as well as original cards and dice of the period.

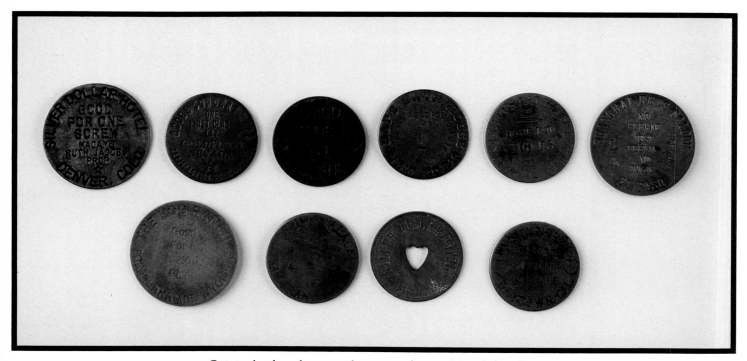

Original whorehouse tokens, as shown "Good for One Screw." *Jonathan Peck.*

Playtime on the frontier! Items include playing cards in a fitted leather case, dice and cup, pocket knife, Jew's harp and set of steamboat playing cards. *Don Spaulding.*

A Jew's harp, circa 1870. *Don Spaulding.*

"Helping to relieve the lonely nights." A small hand concertina dating back to the Civil War. Anyone with musical ability was doubly welcome around the campfire at the end of a long day on the range.

137

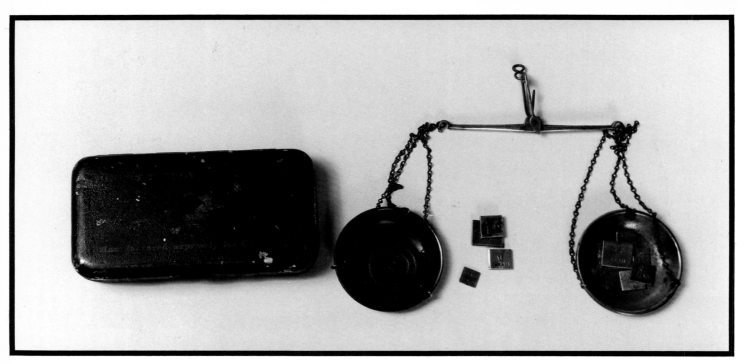

Miniature gold scales with ½ to 3 dram brass counter weights. The lettering on the painted case reads "Miner's improved gold scale—made expressly for California."

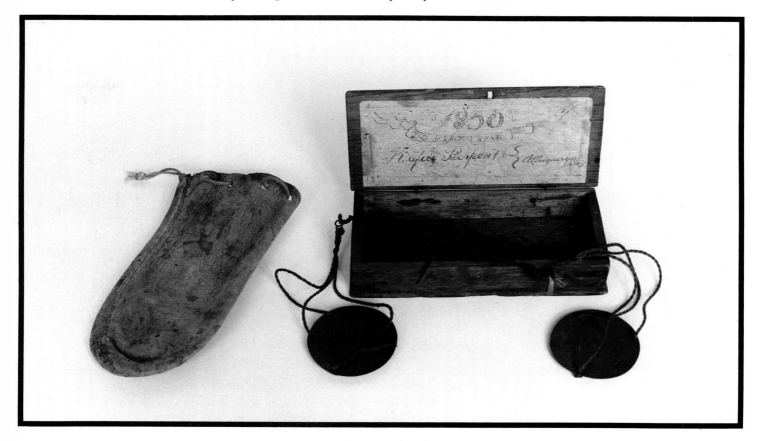

An interesting relic is this set of gold scales in it's original box. The set is dated 1850 and named to Rufus Pierpont of Albuquerque, New Mexico. To the left of the scales is an original gold poke bag. *Don Spaulding*.

Miner's gold pan and shovel, with a sign removed from a mine opening in Colorado in 1940. *Eric von Schmidt.*.

Stock certificate of the Baker Silver Mining Co. of Colorado, February 1, 1868.

This watch was given to A.W. von Schmidt for foiling a Walls Fargo Stagecoach holdup. His great grandson tells me that the "hero" was a passenger in the stagecoach when the dismounted bandit accosted the coach. The driver stopped and raised his hands. Von Schmidt, seeing what transpired, started to exit the stage from the far side, gun in hand. His weight made the coach rock, causing the bandit to avert his eyes from the driver, who seized the moment and lashed the horses, leaving von Schmidt and the bandit facing each other in the dust. The bandit became terrified and bolted on foot—leaving our hero in the middle of the road with his horse tied to a tree. He never returned for the animal, but someone came back 3 days later and found the horse had eaten the bark off the tree for sustinence.

The watch reads:

> Presented to Col. A.W. von Schmidt as a tribute to his gallantry in successfully resisting at the peril of his life, the demand of a highwayman for Wells Fargo & Co. Treasure Box and contents on Quincy Stage, near Live Yankee Ranch, Cal.

Aug. 17th 1875   Lloyd Tevis, Prest.
                                         18 K

An older A.W. von Schmidt.

A young A.W. von Schmidt.

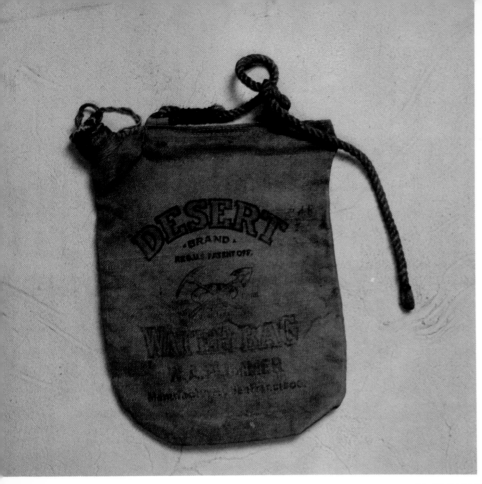

"Desert" brand water bag with corked spout and carrying rope.

"Desert" water bag with miner's sluice pan.

The large vessel is a "gaboon," while the smaller vessel is the more frequently encountered "spittoon," as used in frontier saloons. *Jonathan Peck.*

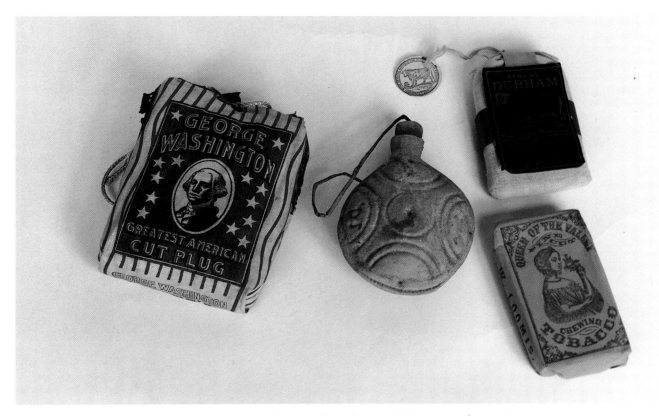

Various types of original smoking and chewing tobacco; in the center is a very rare leather tobacco flask from the Southwest. *Don Spaulding.*

Two hand-carved pipes with pouches of tobacco. *Steve Crowley.*

Tobacco pouch and original tobacco with the "Macho" brand name of "STUD." Produced by the R.J. Reynolds Tobacco Co.

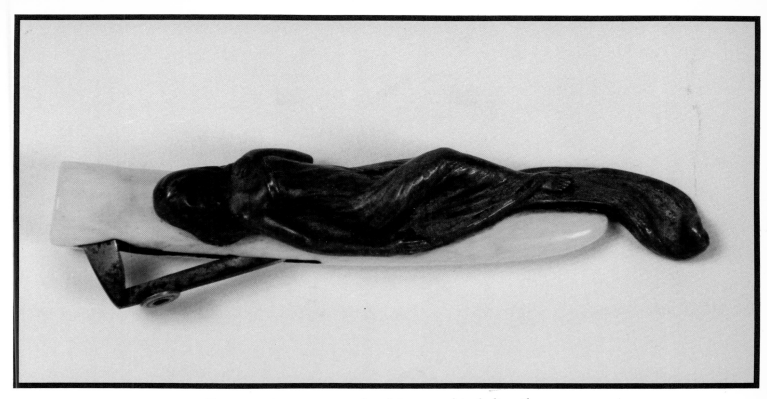

Exquisite cigar cutter made of ivory and including the draped figure of a female. *Jonathan Peck.*

Three of the brands of chewing tobacco often encountered in the West. *Don Spaulding.*

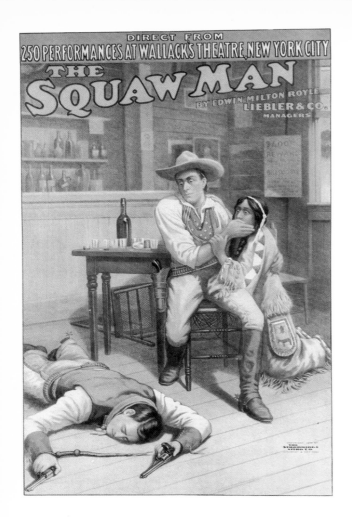

Theatre poster from the movie "The Squaw Man."

Lone Star Harry Memorabilia. This outstanding lot contains Lone Star Harry's cartridge belt and holster both initialed L. S. H. on a brass plate, a Colt Single Action Army smokeless .38 center fire pistol with stag grips, a working presentation pocket watch inscribed to him from the Wild West Show, a piece of his personal stationery, a photograph of Lone Star Harry with friends and Indian Bill's Wild West Wagon in the background, along with a pamphlet about Lone Star Harry, American Representative Scout, known as the Revolver King. *Jerard Paul Jordan Galleries/M.L. Gardner Photography.*

Program from the 1912 presentation of the Buffalo Bill
Rough Rider Show in Norwich, Connecticut.

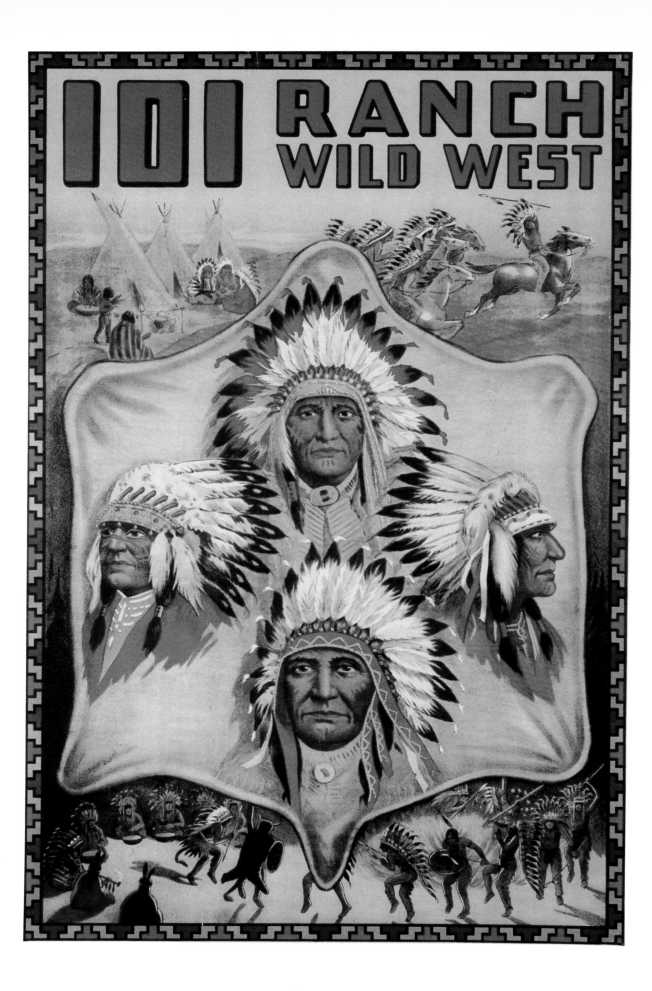

Buffalo Bill & Indian Chief

WM. NOTMAN & SON—MONTREAL.

Opposite page:
Poster from the 101 Ranch Wild West Show; this was purchased in 1965 from one of the last surviving riders performing in the show.

Above:
Cabinet photo of Buffalo Bill and Sitting Bull who joined the Cody Wild West Show in 1884.

Buffalo Bill program with historical sketches.

A great 47" long photo of the 101 Wild West Show, the successors to the Buffalo Bill Wild West Show. This shot was taken about 1915, and included in the center of the shot are Chief Iron Tail who posed for the Buffalo nickel, as well as Jess Willard, Heavyweight Boxing Champion of the World.

"Christopher (Kit) Carson. made a Master Mason in Monteruma Lodge No. 1, AF + AM, dec. 26th, 1854. Died at Fort Lyons, Colorado, May 23rd, 1868; buried at Taos, New Mexico." Print from original glass plate negative. *Robert Dailey.*

Signed Buffalo Bill cabinet photo, with the signature on the back of the photo.

The reverse side of Buffalo Bill's cabinet photo. In Buffalo Bill's handwriting is a dedication to Edith Helen Gunderson, Boston, Mass., June 18, 1895, and signed "Buffalo Bill."

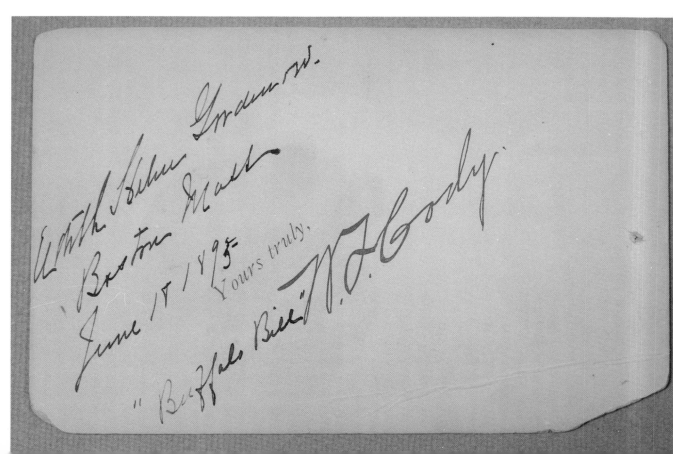

Cabinet photo of a typical Western type with rifle and pistol. Denver, Colorado.

Cabinet photo of a typical young cowboy with lariat and pistol. Laramie, Wyoming.

Buffalo horn clock, made by Albert Fredick. He was the owner of the Black Horn Saloon, Texas, circa 1910. *Don Spaulding.*

Carpet bags from the Civil War era. *Don Spaulding.*

Burial tag of the Bureau of Indian Affairs, Wyoming Territory. *Larry Kaufman.*

Rope maker. This was set on the top rail of a fence, separate lines were secured to the three different attachments and the handle was cranked to produce rope. *Jonathan Peck.*

A composite photo of a "Mountain Man" trapper's gear, showing clockwise from the top, a cooking kettle, trap, carved wooden water cup (slung from the belt), metal fire striker, and trade ax. Resting on the sash is the trapper's clay pipe. *Don Spaulding.*

A Civil War era picket pin and rope, with horse hubbles in the foreground. *Don Spaulding.*

Watch fob with miniature Nevada marshal's badge. *Jonathan Peck.*

Our western tradition! A pulp magazine cover of "Western Story," 1924.

Titled "Secrets of the Desert" by Carl Hantman. A preliminary oil sketch done as a study prior to the final painting. Carl Hantman is famous for his Apache paintings, and is considered a "painter's painter." His work is immediately snapped up by collectors as soon as it is finished.

Painting titled "Return of the War Party" by Harold Von Schmidt. His career spanned fifty productive years, mostly for the *Saturday Evening Post*. He was one of the rare artists who could create life-like scenes without the aid of a camera. He used his two sons, Peter and Eric, as models for many of his paintings. Considered the modern day Frederick Remington. Oil on Canvas. *Eric Von Schmidt.*

Leather Goods Makers

It would be impossible to accurately list all leather workers in the West, so we will note those whose work was outstanding and highly desirable to collectors.

Arizona Saddlery Co., Prescott, Arizona. Owned by Frank Olzer. Saddles.

Askew Bros., Kansas City, Kansas. 1866-1910.

Blickhahn & Co., Medicine Lodge, Kansas.

Cogshall, C.E., Montana. Saddles and chaps.

Collins, G.H. and J.S., Cheyenne, Wyoming. Saddles and gun rigs. Sold in 1896 to A.Q. Cornish.

Donnel, J.A., Rawlins, Wyoming. Saddles.

Flynn, T., Pueblo, Colorado. Saddles.

Frazier, R.F., Pueblo, Colorado. Worked for P. Becker, Leadville, CO., and S.C. Gallup in Pueblo, acquiring the firm in 1897. The company continued until the mid-1940s. Chaps, cuffs, gun rigs, and saddles.

Furstnow, A.F., Miles City, Montana. Chaps and gun rigs. Established in 1884 and the originator of the "Miles City Saddle." Produced a full line of saddles, saddle trees, stirrups, cuffs, holsters, and belts, as well as Tapaderos, chaps and quirts.

Gallup, S.C., Pueblo, Colorado. Early saddle-maker, noted for chaps and saddles.

Hamley and Co., Pendleton, Oregon. Began in 1883 in Ashton, South Dakota and moved to Pendleton in June, 1905. Large saddlery company noted for saddles, quirts, chaps, and skirts. First catalog published in 1909.

Jenkins and Son, Salt Lake City, Utah. Est. 1855. Known for their saddles.

Keyston Bros., San Francisco, California. Est. 1868. The largest West Coast saddlery; associated with Main and Winchester 1867. Bought out J.C. Johnson and L.D. Stone, successors to Main and Winchester. Merged in 1954 with H.H. Heiser Co. Known for saddles, holsters, whips, etc.

Lawrence, G. and Co., Portland, Oregon. Est. 1893. Belts, chaps, gun rigs, saddles, and tack.

Main and Winchester, San Francisco, California. Circa 1849. Acquired by Keyston Bros. 1912. Gun rigs. Considered the most famous of the California firms. Standardized the now famous "California Style" holsters.

Meanea, F., Cheyenne, Wyoming. Circa 1870. Noted craftsman, famous for his careful work. Chaps, gun rigs, holsters, saddles, and saddle scabbards.

Meldrum, R., Rawlins, Wyoming. Gun rigs and saddles.

Miles City Saddlery Co., Miles City, Montana. Successor to the Cogshall Saddle Co. Gun rigs and saddles.

Mueller, F., Denver, Colorado. 1883 to the 1940s. Saddles and gun rigs.

Myres, S.D., El Paso, Texas. 1897 to the 1980s. Saddles and gun rigs.

Pickard, W.L. and Sons, Phoenix, Arizona. Original makers of the Pony Express saddles, as well as gun rigs.

Porter, N., Phoenix, Arizona. Started the business in Texas in 1875, but moved to Phoenix in 1895. Saddles and cuffs.

Price, L., Tulsa, Indian Territory.

Read, J.G. and Sons, Ogden, Utah. Bought Hodman Saddlery in 1883 and existed into the 1980s. Saddlery and tack.

Searle Saddlery, Vernal, Utah. Saddle scabbards.

Sears Roebuck and Co., Chicago, Illinois. Gun rigs.

Snyder Saddles, Denver, Colorado. Saddles, chaps, and cuffs.

Sweat, D.L., Hugo, Oklahoma.

Thompson, W.R., Rifle, Colorado. A Western Slope saddlery firm. 1888 to 1941. Saddles and saddle-makers tools.

Visalia Stock Saddle Co., San Francisco, California. Founded Visalia, California, 1870, by D.E. Walker and Henry Shuham; acquired by Edmund Weeks, 1899, and moved to San Francisco. Saddles and gun rigs.

Western Saddle Manufacturing Co., Denver, Colorado. Successors (1919) to J.H. Wilson Saddlery, est. 1885. Saddles and saddle scabbards.

Wilson, A.E., Tulsa, Indian Territory.

Bibliography

Antique Guns, Hank Wieand Bowman, Fawcett Books, 1956.

The Atchison Saddlery Co., Illustrative and Descriptive Catalog and Price List, Number 12, 1923, Atchison, Kansas.

Cavalry Wife, The Diary of Eveline M. Alexander, 1866-1867, Edited by Sandra L. Myres, Texas A & M University Press, 1977.

Cowboy and Gunfighter Collectibles, Bill Mackin, Mountain Press Publishing Co., Missoula, 1989.

The Cowboy, Phillip A. Rollins, Charles Scribner's Sons, 1922.

The Cowboy, Vincent Paul Rennert, Crowell-Collier Press, 1966.

The Cowboy Catalog, Sandra Kauffman, Clarkson Potter, 1980.

Guns Of The World, Hans Tanner, Ed., Bonanza Books, Div. of Crown Publishing Co., 1977.

Catalog #82, North & Judd Manufacturing Company, New Britain, Connecticut, 1909.

The Old West: The Cowboys, Time-Life Books, 1973.

Old West Antiques & Collectibles, Great American Publishing Company, Austin, Texas, 1979.

Picture History Of The Wild West, James D. Horan, Crown, 1954.

The Sharps Rifle, It's History, Development and Operation, Winstonn O. Smith, William Morrow & Co., 1943.

The Texas Rangers, Walter P. Webb, Houghton-Mifflin, 1935.

The United States Cavalry, An Illustrated History, Gregory J.W. Urwin, Blandford Press, 1983.

COWBOY COLLECTIBLES AND WESTERN MEMORABILIA

VALUE GUIDE

Due to the numerous variables involved in valuing individual pieces of any collection, we have used the following guide for the items shown in the book. At the request of several collectors, we have not assigned a value to a number of the outstanding pistols shown.

A - up to $100.00
B - $100.00 to $250.00
C - $250.00 to $500.00
D - $500.00 to $750.00

E - $750.00 to $1,000.00
F - $1,000.00 to $2,500.00
G - $2,500.00 to $5,000.00

H - $5,000.00 to $7,500.00
I - $7,500.00 to $10,000.00
J - In excess of $10,000.00